Laughter is the
Best Weapon

Laughter is the Best Weapon

The Remarkable Adventures of an Unconventional Soldier

Charles Ritchie

Pen & Sword
MILITARY

First published in Great Britain in 2021 and reprinted in 2021 by
Pen & Sword Military
An imprint of
Pen & Sword Books Ltd
Yorkshire – Philadelphia

ISBN 978 1 39909 188 6

Typeset by Mac Style
Printed and bound in the UK by CPI Group (UK) Ltd,
Croydon, CR0 4YY

Pen & Sword Books Limited incorporates the imprints of Atlas,
Archaeology, Aviation, Discovery, Family History, Fiction, History,
Maritime, Military, Military Classics, Politics, Select, Transport,
True Crime, Air World, Frontline Publishing, Leo Cooper, Remember
When, Seaforth Publishing, The Praetorian Press, Wharncliffe
Local History, Wharncliffe Transport, Wharncliffe True Crime
and White Owl.

For a complete list of Pen & Sword titles please contact

PEN & SWORD BOOKS LIMITED
47 Church Street, Barnsley, South Yorkshire, S70 2AS, England
E-mail: enquiries@pen-and-sword.co.uk
Website: www.pen-and-sword.co.uk

Or

PEN AND SWORD BOOKS
1950 Lawrence Rd, Havertown, PA 19083, USA
E-mail: Uspen-and-sword@casematepublishers.com
Website: www.penandswordbooks.com

For my darling first wife Araminta and our loving son Paul

Contents

Her Royal Highness The Princess Royal

While Colonel in Chief of The Royal Scots I was often asked, by people who know him, how on earth Charles Ritchie managed to rise to the rank of Brigadier and then became Colonel of The Regiment. Even now, despite having known Charles for almost 50 years, I can only assume it was right place, right time or through a series of fortunate computer errors and mistaken identity.

To say he has had an unusual life would be a gross understatement. He is the only man I know with the bare-faced charm to have used whisky to inveigle the President of the USA into his office in Melbourne for a private meeting; the outrageous luck to have survived being run over by an eight-wheeled Russian missile launcher; and the incredible stupidity to have swum with venomous sea-snakes, accidentally poisoned himself with cyanide in Libya and got blown up by his own troops in Yemen.

His military career has taken him all over the world and introduced him to Presidents and Dictators, popstars and politicians, heroes and villains. As a result, at numerous social events over the years, Charles has entertained countless people (myself included) with wonderful anecdotes of his colourful life in the Army. I am therefore delighted that he has finally put these stories together in this book, for all to enjoy – and very grateful to him for donating a share of the proceeds to 'Save the Children'.

Anne

Chapter 1

To Be or Not to Be?

As a boy, I had no interest in joining the Army. My inspiration as a child was Pat Cox, headmaster of Durlston Court, a preparatory school in Hampshire where I was sent as a bewildered nine-year-old. Pat Cox had been a Captain in the Grenadier Guards during the First World War and would march through the dining room blowing his whistle and shouting the headlines of the day, such as 'Stalin is dead!', 'The Korean War is over' and 'England are 122 for 3!'

More interestingly for me, he loved amateur dramatics and, as a result, school plays were a regular part of the curriculum. One of the school's most famous Old Boys, the wonderful comedic actor Tony Hancock, always maintained that his acting career was initiated at Durlston and nurtured by Pat Cox's enthusiasm and encouragement.

Hancock's time at Durlston preceded mine by many years. Nevertheless, even as he became more famous, he always stayed in touch with the school. At the height of his fame, with *Hancock's Half Hour* in full swing on British TV, he still came to see the big school production each year.

He therefore had the privilege of seeing me in my formative years at ages twelve and thirteen, playing the female lead in two plays, *The Ghost Train* and *The Happiest Days of Your Life*, and was kind enough to stick around after each performance and chat to us young actors. I vividly remember him saying to me that if I ever wanted to go on the stage as a career I should look him up.

And so I did. Four years later, when I was seventeen and trying to decide what to do with my life I went to see him in a theatre in London, having got in touch via our old headmaster at Durlston. My question to him was simple: to be or not to be an actor?

He had very firm advice for me.

'Look here, young fellow, you have some talent. But talent has nothing to do with it. It's luck that's the important thing.'

'Luck?'

'Yes, luck. I couldn't recommend acting as a career to anyone.'

'Oh ...'

'Can you name the world's two highest paid film actors?'

'Er ...'

'I'll tell you. John Wayne and David Niven. Neither can act to save his life. They just walk on and off screen as themselves.'

Feeling rather deflated, I explained that the alternative was to fall in line with my father's wishes and follow him into a career in the Army, as I had been offered a place at Sandhurst. He considered this for a moment.

'Well, I was in the military for a while, you know. If I were you, I'd join up. I think you'll find that being a natural actor will be very useful in the Army.'

That seemed pretty clear advice to me, and since it came from such a famous and successful individual, I took him at his word. The next day I accepted the offer from Sandhurst.

Yes, mother, Tony Hancock made me do it.

*　　*　　*

Germany declared war on the USA on 11 December 1941. Within 24 hours, Britain produced an immediate military response, in the shape of – me. My mother, flushed with patriotic fever, gave birth to her first-born in Inverness General Hospital.

My father was not present at my birth. Lieutenant Colonel Bill MacIver-Ritchie of The Royal Scots (The Royal Regiment) had the good sense to stay well away, although getting posted to Hong Kong was a little extreme. Fortunately for him and us, he happened to be shipped back to Staff College in Camberley shortly before Hong Kong was attacked by the Japanese and the 1st Battalion of The Royal Scots was, effectively, wiped out.

While my father was preoccupied with the war, we lived at Ardlarach, a large, cold, stone farmhouse in the remote Scottish Highlands. Imagine James Bond's *Skyfall* but with much less glamour. My paternal grandfather, Colonel Charles William MacIver-Ritchie of The Royal Horse Artillery, had retired to live there with his wife and three children – my father Bill and his two sisters, Rosemary and Dawn. My grandfather was one of only two of his intake at the Royal Military Academy at Woolwich to have survived the First World War, so he didn't notice a bit of discomfort, even while the rest of the family broke icicles to keep warm. One of my earliest memories is lying in bed trying to stop myself shivering, while I watched bats flitting around the room and selfishly adding to the draughts.

My mother Iris was the daughter of Commander Douglas Murray of the Royal Navy, whose family history of unbroken naval service went back as far as Admiral George Murray, Nelson's Captain of Fleet. Lacking a battleship of her own, my mother did her bit for the war effort by being a 'Land Girl', working all hours on our farm, so my early military training as a toddler was at the feet of my formidable granny.

My first contact with soldiers involved a group from the Norwegian Army who lived in temporary accommodation on our land at the end of the drive. The officers were regular visitors and would entertain the ladies of the house with singing and dancing. Aunt Dawn married the one with the best voice.

I developed a skill for impersonation very early in my childhood or, to be more precise, an ability to employ the accent and dialect of whomever I spoke to. I found this very useful for translating when some of the local children came up to the farm, which was quite often. Maybe they were drawn by my sparkling personality at such a young age, or more likely because in those days of strict rationing, we had plenty of vegetables, fruit and eggs.

'Charles, kin ye ask yer granny if ah kin hae anither o' thae wee biscuits?'

'Aye, okay Jeannie, ah'll ask ma granny.'

'Grandmother, is it alright if Jeannie has another scone?'

'Yes, Charles, of course it is.'

'Thank you, grandmother.'

'Aye, Jeannie, ma granny sez thit ye can hae anither wee biscuit.'

* * *

In 1943, after the Italian Armistice, my father was posted to the sunshine of the Mediterranean, as Staff Officer to the garrison commander on the previously Italian-controlled island of Leros.

Leros was very much in demand as a destination, due to its strategic military importance in the Mediterranean and its excellent sunbathing facilities. The Germans invaded in force but, unlike their modern tactic of putting towels on sunbeds the night before, they sent Stukas and paratroopers. Over three days and nights my father took part in a spirited but ultimately unsuccessful defence of the island and was eventually reported as killed in action.

I was too young to appreciate the awful news at the time but learned later that the local community was very supportive of my mother and even organized the installation of a commemorative plaque outside the local church. This had to be removed a few months later, when a letter from the Red Cross arrived stating that my father had actually been wounded and taken prisoner.

He spent the next eighteen months in a variety of PoW camps but finally returned home safe and sound when the war ended. Thereafter, my mother would regularly remind him that she blamed the Red Cross for stopping her remarrying a handsome singing Norwegian.

* * *

My earliest memory of my father was the day of his return to Scotland after the war. We met him off the train at Inverness Railway Station and had lunch in the Station Hotel. He took me by the hand for a visit to the bathroom, and I remember excitedly running back to my mother across the lobby of the hotel.

'Mummy, mummy, you'll never guess what!'

'Ssssh, don't shout. What is the matter?'

'Daddy has just spent a penny into a basin!'

I had of course never been into a 'Gents' in my life and assumed that the white basins attached to the wall at about shoulder height were for washing one's hands in.

* * *

In 1946 my father was posted as Acting Commanding Officer of the 2nd Battalion The Royal Scots to Malta, and my mother and I sailed on board the troopship *Dunera* to join him.

The island used to be the winter residence of my great-great-grandfather, Charles MacIver. His older brother, David MacIver, had started a shipping company in 1838 with Sam Cunard and Robert Napier ('the father of Clyde shipbuilding') which they blessed with the snappy title of 'The British and North American Royal Mail Steam Packet Company'. After David's death, Charles and Sam expanded the company with great success, although it wasn't renamed 'The Cunard Steamship Company' until 1878 after Charles sold his share.

When I was older, I asked my father where all the money had gone that had forced us to take on the life of salaried gypsies, which is what I consider Army life to be. Apparently, Charlies MacIver invested all the money from selling his share of Cunard in an ambitious project to build railways throughout Argentina, but it unfortunately hit the buffers quite spectacularly and he lost the lot.

The eagle-eyed amongst you, or at least those still awake, might have noticed that my father and grandfather both had the rather grand double-barrelled surname of MacIver-Ritchie, whereas I do not. When Charles MacIver's daughter Jane married my great-grandfather William Ritchie, Charles insisted that the couple combine surnames so that his family name would not be lost.

When I was born my father was away serving in the war, so my mother registered my birth herself. My parents had agreed that, if they had a son, he would be called Charles David MacIver-Ritchie, but my dear mother wrote my name down on the register incorrectly:

FORENAMES: Charles David MacIver
SURNAME: Ritchie

My great-great-grandfather must have been spinning in his hammock.

*   *   *

After nine months in Malta, 2nd Battalion The Royal Scots moved to Trieste, with my father still as acting Commanding Officer. We moved into a splendid flat on the fourth floor of an imposing apartment block that overlooked the Piazza Oberdan, where we lived for over three years. We had two staff – a maid/nanny called Ardea and the most fabulous cook called Anna. When I say 'fabulous' I do not refer to her cooking. My mother reminded me many years later of a conversation she had with me.

'Mummy, Anna has just shown me her fantastic fur coat.'

'Oh yes, dear?'

'Yes. I bet you she didn't buy it.'

My mother was nervous that I had acquired knowledge inappropriate for a child of such tender years.

'What do you mean, darling?'

'I mean one of her boyfriends must have bought it for her'.

Indeed, Anna's daily urgency to serve dinner as quickly as possible before rushing out was a matter of some concern, but what she did in her spare time was surely up to her.

*   *   *

Trieste was the location of my first military action, aged eight, when my love of pyrotechnics caused me to destroy a 3-ton British Army truck, although I blame the driver for having parked his lorry underneath the Dukes' flat.

The Dukes were our neighbours on the other side of the stairs. Our parents were attending some important Garrison event and, with Ardea the maid otherwise engaged for the evening, their nanny was looking after their sons Tobin and Johnny as well as yours truly.

To keep ourselves amused we were making paper darts. I came up with the brilliant idea of setting fire to them and launching them off the balcony into the open air above the street. This was tremendous fun as they flew magnificently for a few seconds before dropping in a ball of fire. It was unfortunate that the largest paper dart of the day, as the flames caught hold, crash-landed on the canvas roof of the parked lorry. To our horror, the canvas started to collapse in flames on to the wooden seats and floorboards, and within seconds the whole lorry was ablaze.

Panicking, we closed the balcony windows, destroyed the evidence of dart-making, placed the matches back on the mantelpiece and started a frantic game of Ludo. When our parents returned, they were somewhat bemused to see the local fire brigade dousing the smouldering remains of an army truck at the entrance to the apartment block.

*   *   *

Held in good repair in nearby Duino Castle was a magnificent six-wheeled German staff car that had been used by Rommel.

At one point there was a transport crisis, and vehicles had to be requisitioned to take children to and from school. I happened to be staying with my friend Robert Parsons, whose father was the Chief of Staff to General Sir Terence Airy at Duino Castle, and for several days we were taken to school in this monstrous vehicle. Italian heads turned to stare at the sight of this huge car with a motley collection of schoolboys waving from the back seat.

The car was used later by Field Marshal Montgomery on a visit to Trieste. I was allowed to hold the door open for him – the first recorded occasion of my expertise at crawling to a senior officer.

* * *

The best thing about Trieste was the availability of cap guns. They came in all sizes and fired either rolls of paper caps or the little metal caps that you placed in the chamber over a small spike, which when hit with the pistol 'hammer' let off the most realistic bang.

The greatest fun of all were the brown paper 'grenades' that were roughly the size of a ping-pong ball. They appeared to contain small pieces of gravel mixed with black powder and were wrapped in brown paper and fastened with thin wire. When thrown hard down on to the pavement or against a wall they exploded with an impressive flash and the noise of a pistol being discharged.

One Saturday afternoon, I was playing with Johnny and Tobin Duke in our flat when we heard a major disturbance going on in the main street around the corner. Pausing to grab a bag of 'grenades', we ran up to the flat roof. On the street below was a formation of riot police, several rows deep, supported by lorries mounted with water cannon. Facing them was a crowd of several thousand protesting about something or other – a regular occurrence in those days.

On this occasion the confrontation was peaceful which, as a spectacle, was rather boring. We decided it might be fun to liven up the proceedings by hurling a handful of 'grenades' on to the street. The plan was to throw them into the open space between the opposing parties, but we had not allowed for the wind. Our 'grenades', caught in the breeze, drifted towards the police.

We watched in horror as the grenades exploded on helmets and around feet. There was obvious alarm amongst the police, who thought they were being attacked, but it was the reaction of the crowd that caused the panic. They mistook the noise and flashes for the police opening fire on them, and total chaos followed as hysterical people tried to flee the area.

We did not stay around to watch what happened, as we suspected we had been spotted by the constabulary, who no doubt put out a general alert for three dwarf anarchists seen hurling explosives. We rushed back into the flat and started another frantic game of Ludo before the police stormed up the stairs. We just got away with it, but some close questioning the following day from Signor Battalini, the hall porter, made it clear that he had a pretty good idea who the 'anarchists of restricted growth' had been.

*　*　*

I was sent in September 1951 to preparatory school at Durlston Court, which brings me back to where I began this opening chapter and where my love of acting the fool was established.

As well as drama, Durlston was also notable for having a drill squad armed with genuine Martini-Henry bolt-action rifles. They had been 'acquired' by Pat Cox at the end of the First World War and, not surprisingly, we boys loved them.

At weekends we would go and help ourselves to the rifles, which were casually stored in a cupboard under the stage in the school hall. We would usually split into two opposing camps: the French Foreign Legion and the Arabs. All this was modelled on *Luck of the Legion* which appeared each week in the only comic we were allowed, the *Eagle*.

Each Legionnaire would fold in the rims of his grey sun hat, leaving just a peak at the front, whilst a white handkerchief would be tucked under the back, giving a passable impression of a Legion *kepi*. Each Arab would drape a towel over his head and secure it in place with a trouser belt. The French Foreign Legion lived in home-made wooden forts, whilst the Arabs lived in tents.

On most Sunday afternoons throughout the summer, raiding parties scurried around, battles raged, prisoners were taken and a peace conference was held just before the bell sounded for the Juniors to go to bed. Little did I know back then that, just a few short years later, I would visit real French Foreign Legion forts and be shot at by real Arabs.

*　*　*

In 1955, while I was still at Durlston, my parents moved to Ismailia in Egypt, on the west bank of the Suez Canal, which was still under British Protection, with the French Canal Company operating the canal itself.

We used to fly to Egypt from Blackbushe Airport near Camberley in Surrey, on a Dan Air Avro York. These four-engined aircraft incorporated many of the features of the Lancaster bomber and had a cruising speed of only around 200mph and a top speed of just 300mph. Hence it took a whole day to fly to the Faid Royal Air Force base in the Canal Zone, with refuelling stops both on Malta and at El Adem in Libya.

At the end of one holiday, we got to the airport for the flight back to England only to be told that one of the two aircraft had 'gone U.S.' (Un Serviceable) – a phrase that, with apologies to my many American friends, I use to this day as it seems to become ever more appropriate.

The decision was taken that the 'Lollipop Special' taking school children would be the second priority flight – the one serviceable aircraft would first be used to take RAF personnel going back to the UK on leave. Parents objected at this enforced extension of their parenting obligations, none more so than General Sir Richard Hull, the Commander in Chief of the Middle East, whose son was on the school flight. However, even he cut no ice with the RAF Movements Flight Lieutenant.

We therefore got an extra day of holiday. How shocked everybody subsequently was when the news came in the next day. The one serviceable Dan Air Avro York, which we should have been on, had crashed into the sea shortly after taking off from Malta with the loss of all on board.

* * *

My father was keen for me to follow him and my grandfather and forge a career in the British Army. As I approached the age of thirteen, he decided I should go to a more military-based boarding school and, as he was still a serving officer, he had the opportunity to pay reduced rates to send me to Wellington College in Berkshire.

It was indeed a very military-minded school with an active Cadet Force, allowing us to play with all manner of guns and things, which was great fun. However, it also had an Amateur Dramatics group. The gypsy life of a soldier's son, always moving to new countries and hearing new languages and accents, had honed my skill in mimicry. Whether it was with Italians in Trieste, or Arabs in Egypt, I learned not just some vocabulary but also, crucially, the correct local accent. The stage gave me plenty of opportunity to show this off.

In my second term I got a role in the school's production of *Journey's End*. The play depicts life in an officers' trench during the First World War. My parents came to the opening night, and we chatted together afterwards. My father was positively beaming.

'Well, lad – that is a fine play. It really shows what it means to be an officer in the British Army. The courage, the honour and the dignity.'

'Yes, father. I really enjoyed taking part.'

'I hope it's helped to underline what you should do with your life?'

'Yes, father. I want to be an actor.'

*   *   *

I enjoyed my time at Wellington and in my final year, aged seventeen, I was made the 'Head of The Hill' by the housemaster – Hill House being my house throughout my years at the College. As Head Boy I could lord it over the other students somewhat, given that I was responsible for discipline and time-keeping.

Discipline was strict at Wellington, and in my younger years I was several times on the receiving end of 'six of the best'. However, as Head of The Hill, I occasionally administered this punishment on behalf of our housemaster. I even had to beat my great friend Robert Parsons, who had committed the heinous crime of swearing.

I played Rugby for the 3rd XV. Yes, I was that good. They put me out on the wing because, when scared, I could run like the wind. I was also a keen Colour Sergeant in the Combined Cadet Force. The highlight of each term was our 'Field Day', when we were taken to Salisbury Plain and allowed to run around playing at being real soldiers.

It is amazing that no boy was ever killed on a field day, as they always ended in a magnificent set-piece battle. The chosen lucky one in each section of ten boys was given a Bren gun with a magazine of thirty rounds of balsa wood 'bullets'. When fired, these bullets hit a blank firing attachment at the end of the barrel which pulverised them into tiny fragments that came out in an impressive sheet of flame with an ear-shattering bang.

The rest of us had to remain content with firing blanks from our .303 bolt action rifles. One year, a group of us experimented by placing the top half-inch of a sharpened pencil into the breech, in order to simulate a bullet. I shudder now to think of the terrible consequences had these home-made bullets ever found a vital organ or an eye.

Despite all the war games at Wellington, I continued to pursue my love of amateur dramatics. My mother was quite relaxed about my intention to take to the stage. She herself was a great mimic of voices and mannerisms, she could act and sing and she always loved being the centre of attention at parties. I am so like her.

* * *

I harboured a sneaking wish to join Cunard and restore the family fortunes, so I arranged for an interview at Cunard's HQ in Liverpool. With my ancestry I fully expected to be welcomed with open arms and given a plum job, but it quickly went pear-shaped instead.

Having marched in, bold as brass, I explained to the personnel manager that I was a direct descendant of Charles MacIver and therefore felt that it must be in my blood to be a great success with the company. Destiny, and all that.

My interviewer was not impressed.

'I don't give a stuff who your great-great-grandfather was. You'll start at the bottom like everyone else. If you're any good, you'll work your way up. If not, you'll still be making tea in this office when you retire.'

I thanked him very much for his time and returned to Wellington, my plan to be the family's next shipping magnate holed beneath the waterline.

* * *

It was then that I took up an invitation from the Army, organized by my father, to attend the Regular Commissions Board at Westbury, to be assessed for entry to Sandhurst. I still had no desire to join up, but it offered the chance to get away from school for three days, with free rail travel from Crowthorne station and unrestricted access to the local hostelries. Too good an opportunity for a seventeen-year-old to miss!

In fact, I had such a carefree attitude to the whole process that, instead of being nervous or apprehensive like many of the other candidates, I found the three days to be great fun. I got stuck in to all the various initiative tests and leadership assessments, engaged enthusiastically with all the interviewers and in the evenings, joined all the other candidates in the local pub for drinks.

At the end of the third day I was sent for by the course leader.

'Ah, Ritchie, come in – sit down.'

'Thank you, Sir.'

'Tell me, how has it been for you here?'

'I've thoroughly enjoyed it, thank you.'

'Yes, but how well do you think you have done?'

'Oh, I don't know, Sir.'

There was a grumpy silence while he tried to work out if I was playing it cool or was genuinely a fool.

'Oh, well, congratulations anyway, Ritchie. You have passed the Officer's Selection Board. How soon do you want to start at Sandhurst?'

I hadn't really thought this through and was temporarily lost for words.

'Well, boy? When do you want to start?

'Er … I don't, Sir.'

'What do you mean, you don't?!'

'I don't actually want to go to Sandhurst. I only came to have a bit of fun and get away from school.'

The course leader took a moment to regain his composure and then barked at me to stay exactly where I was, while he marched out of the room.

He soon returned, in no better a mood.

'Ritchie – the Commandant wants to see you. Follow me.'

I was marched into the Commandant's office.

'Ritchie, is it? What is this I hear about you wasting our valuable time?'

'With respect, Sir, I have learned a great deal here at Westbury and have thoroughly enjoyed the experience, so I do not think anyone's time has been wasted.'

'But you don't want to go to Sandhurst?'

'No, Sir.'

There was another of those angry silences. Finally, the Commandant spoke again.

'Right, Ritchie, here are your papers with the offer to enter Sandhurst. It's valid for one year. Now get out.'

Chapter 2

The Darling Buds of Inkerman

I was delighted when my schoolboy friend Robert Parsons also turned up as an Officer Cadet at the Royal Military Academy Sandhurst (RMAS), in a later intake to mine. Robert had grown somewhat and now stood at an impressive 6′ 6″, practically twice my height.

Robert acquired a 1938 Morgan sports car while at Sandhurst, for the princely sum of £100. He had to fold himself in two to get into it. The brakes only worked every other day, but we could never remember which.

The Morgan came to grief in the suburbs of Camberley, while heavily overloaded with passengers on our day off. It was unfortunately also an off-day for the brakes, and so a rather tight bend and excess speed combined to defeat Robert's driving skills. The car hit the pavement sideways with sufficient force to crack the wooden chassis and it ended up bent like a banana. We only got it back to RMAS by constantly shifting our weight so that we had three wheels on the ground at any one time.

* * *

Sandhurst has three Colleges: Old College, in front of which they hold the Sovereign's Parade, where it is said that 'gentlemen come from'; Victory College, where it is said that 'officers come from'; and New College, where 'other ranks came from'. Due to a glaring clerical error, I was put in Old College.

Discipline was unbelievably strict.

'You are an idle officer cadet! That shoelace is untied – extra parade for you, 6.00am tomorrow!'

That said, a freak event occurred during my time at Sandhurst that led to an incredible breakdown in discipline.

Old College never tried to win the Drill competition, which was viewed as an 'other ranks' event. As a result, a formal Old College guest night was always arranged for the same day as the Drill Competition, something the other colleges never did. But on one fateful day, one of the four companies from Old College accidentally won the Drill competition. They must have stopped concentrating or something.

The resulting celebrations quickly got out of control, and we were all sent back to our 'Lines', i.e. our dormitories. Frustrated at the premature end to our party, we rebels in Inkerman Company decided for fun to attack Waterloo Company on the floor beneath us and dropped buckets of water and fireworks down on them. As close neighbours, we then decided to join forces to attack the other two Old College companies, Blenheim and Dettingen, who were on the other side of Chapel Square.

On our way across the Square we met our intended opponents on their way to attack us. After a brief and rather incoherent negotiation, we collectively decided in our drunken state that all four companies of Old College would combine to attack the boringly sober Victory College.

We armed ourselves with a 250-gallon mobile fire extinguisher and the Ritchie Rocket Launcher, which I had invented earlier in the year – a perspex-covered wooden map board with a hole in the middle, into which was placed a piece of metal Hoover tubing, giving its bearer the ability to aim the flight of a firework rocket.

On reaching Victory College we began our assault with a rocket attack on one of the ante rooms. I aimed the Ritchie Rocket Launcher in the general direction of the anteroom and lit a firework. Astonishingly, it flew straight and true, smashed through a window, exploded, and set fire to the curtains.

Mayhem ensued, with hundreds of cadets on both sides throwing fireworks and all sorts at each other, until the duty Sergeant Major came out.

'Gentlemen! Get back to your Lines NOW, or you will all be put under arrest!'

'F*** off!' came the drunken replies.

We promptly charged him, heads down, and he was butted in the stomach and laid out.

New College then joined Victory College, so we were badly outnumbered. They drove us back to our own College, headed by the Chief Instructor, Parachute Major Farrar-Hockley, who led their assault and was seen gleefully punching our cadets in the head.

We eventually got back to our dormitory. By this time, the College Adjutant had concluded that Inkerman Company cadets were the ringleaders. As he was coming up the stairs, he promptly got a bucket of water over his head from yours truly.

That seemed to be the final straw. All the Academy officers gathered together in preparation to charge up the staircase to our floor to arrest us all. In a sudden burst of guilty conscience, we rapidly tidied up and refilled the fire buckets. Every cadet disappeared back to his room and into bed, leaving only the duty Under-Officer wandering the corridors, whistling quietly as if nothing had happened.

The next day, a massive witch-hunt started, but once the scale of the event had become evident, the Academy Commandant decided to drop the investigation and hush the whole thing up, for fear that the press would get hold of the story of the only outright mutiny ever to occur at the Royal Military Academy, Sandhurst.

*   *   *

Car-owning cadets were rare. Richard Murphy was one of my friends in the same intake and was a great ally in getting the two of us transported to and from social engagements outside the Academy. One such social event, however, caused a temporary breakdown in our relationship and very nearly ended my Army career before it had begun.

We had invited two lovely girls from Camberley to a dance one Saturday evening, but I happened to be the senior duty cadet for the day, which meant I was not able to leave until 8.00pm. Richard told me over breakfast not to worry. He would collect the girls first, then come back for me, and we would all head to the party together.

Richard set off, and I hung around the Lines in my role as duty cadet, trying to avoid anything that might require any effort, could escalate into my needing to take any action or, worse still, might extend the need for my presence beyond the allotted time.

Finally, at 8.00pm sharp, I stood waiting in my finest regalia, sharp as a tack and looking forward to the splendid evening ahead with my absolutely charming young date.

At 8.20pm, I was strolling back and forth, tie slightly askew, with mild impatience. That Richard Murphy, what a sort – probably got delayed chatting up one of the mothers, smooth talker that he was.

At 9.00pm, I was pacing to the end wall and back, slapping it in silent fury each time I about-faced, convinced that the useless buffoon Murphy had run his car into a ditch and was now hopelessly trying to thumb a lift.

By 10.00pm I had gone through all possible scenarios in my mind – except, as it turned out, the real one. I had given myself a raging headache, so I retired to the bar for a drink and then went back to my room for an early night.

I was awoken at around 2.00am by Richard stumbling into my room, full of *joie de vivre* of the grape variety, but also muttering humble apologies of a sort. With my headache still present, the relief that he wasn't dead in a ditch rapidly turned to angry indignation that he had clearly enjoyed a much better evening than I. The room rapidly turned blue as I let rip with my most vitriolic curses.

He was temporarily taken aback by my tirade and slumped down on the floor in front of my bed, cross-legged.

'Charles – I've done a bad thing.'

He paused, apparently deciding whether he could lie convincingly to me, or if the truth was the only option. Eventually, he made his decision.

'I received a message this afternoon that my date couldn't make it – a bad cold or something. I went to pick up your girl anyway, intent on at least seeing you all right. But when I saw her, the devil in me took over. I told her that you had been detained at barracks by some military emergency and that you had asked me to escort her to the party instead.'

Of all the scenarios that I had imagined during my evening vigil, this had not been one. I was still coming to terms with this extraordinary breach – of friendship, of trust and possibly of the Geneva Convention – when Richard tried to soften the blow. He stupidly landed a direct hit to the solar plexus instead.

'I must say, Charles, she is indeed a cracking young girl!'

The red mist that had been forming around my head rapidly crystallized, and I saw with stunning clarity what had to be done.

'Richard Murphy, you contemptible bastard, I am challenging you to a duel!'

'What?'

'Firearms, at dawn, with seconds in attendance.'

Once I had calmed down, I realized that my challenge was a tad over-the-top – dawn was far too early. We agreed to meet after lunch.

*   *   *

At 1400 the following day, we walked silently on to 'Barrossa', the Sandhurst training area, each armed with a shotgun. I had chosen Patrick Cardwell-Moore as a second, while Richard had Paddy Manning with him. The agreement was that we would take alternate shots, starting at a distance of 75 yards and advancing one yard after each shot, until blood was drawn. As a nod to civility, we agreed that we would wear tweed caps and bow our heads while our opponent fired, to offer some protection to our eyes from the lead shot.

Richard won the toss of the coin and so got to fire first. At 75 yards, the lead pellets from a size-6 shotgun cartridge can spread pretty wide and slow down considerably. We each manfully took a few stinging pellets to our bare arms as we slowly advanced towards each other, shot by shot. But after almost a dozen shots each, no blood had been spilt, despite the distance between us having been reduced to 50 yards or so.

Suddenly, Richard broke rank and charged at me, yelling some ancient battle cry or other. I tried to reload but he fired from the hip as he approached. I took a few pellets to my right arm which tore the skin and drew blood.

'Ha! Gotcha, Charles! Victory is mine!'

'You bastard, what the hell are you playing at?'

The seconds rushed in to grab us, with Patrick yelling indignantly about disgrace, cheating, ungentlemanly conduct and something about a re-match. Paddy Manning was simply creased up laughing, while his man was unrepentant.

'I had to charge in and finish it, Charles – I was down to my last cartridge!'

Patrick led me away, cursing at Richard and Paddy over his shoulder.

'What outrageous behaviour, Charles. That fellow has to be taught a lesson!'

'Any suggestions?'

'Not sure – but he needs to have the cocky self-confidence scared out of him.'

We had almost reached the end of the path leading back to the lines. We ducked under a bush at the side of the path, beneath a large tree, and I waited for my erstwhile adversary with my shotgun loaded.

He was not far behind us, sauntering down the path with his gun slung over his shoulder as if he had just been on a grouse shoot, with Paddy alongside him. I waited until they were within a few yards of our hiding spot, and then fired over their heads into the tree, bringing a shower of branches and leaves down on the pair of them as they yelled and fell over with shock.

As they picked themselves up, we agreed to an end to hostilities. We shook hands on it and headed back to our rooms, thinking that that was the end of that.

It wasn't.

* * *

The gossip grapevine in Sandhurst runs through every nook and cranny of the veritable institution and, despite our best efforts to keep our duelling activities secret, it wasn't long before the grapevine had spilled its beans, so to speak. The merry sound of shotgun fire on an otherwise quiet Sunday afternoon might also have had something to do with it.

I was ordered to go and see the Company Sergeant Major.

'I hear that you and Mr Murphy have had an altercation which led to an armed duel.'

'That is correct, Sergeant Major.'

'Show me your right arm, please.'

Impressive – the grapevine was even delivering triage reports. I showed the Sergeant Major my right arm which had received the minor wound and, with a resigned sigh, told him the whole story.

Once I had finished, he gave me the news I was fearing.

'Sir – you can't go around having duels at Sandhurst, it's just not right and proper. I am afraid I will have to report you to the Company Commander. If he then reports it to the Commandant then I expect that both you and Mr Murphy will get thrown out of Sandhurst.'

I spent the next 24 hours assuming my Army career was over before it had really begun.

Fortunately, however, the Company Commander took mercy on Richard and me. Presumably due to his poor eyesight, he mistakenly got the impression from our records that we were doing quite well as cadets and so he gave us a verbal bollocking while stating we 'would make fine officers one day.'

* * *

Officer cadets at Sandhurst are encouraged to take part in 'challenging, adventurous' training exercises during leave periods.

Armed with the enthusiasm of youth, four of us volunteered to attend basic parachute training at Base Ecole Troupes Aeroporte (BETAP) at Pau in the French Pyrenees. In those days, French Paratroopers – *Les Paras* – were the elite of the French military, so we jumped (ahem) at the opportunity.

The Officers' Mess at BETAP contained some of the most experienced war-fighting soldiers in Europe, including veterans of the first Indochina war and the ongoing Algerian War of Independence. Deeply impressed, we were cherubs among gladiators.

We joined a group of young French officer cadets who were also going through parachute training. For the first few days this involved the instructors putting a harness on us, throwing us off a tall tower and laughing at our screams.

On our first day off, we decided to try to see a little more of France at the tax-payer's expense. Biarritz was already well known as a luxurious French resort and, thanks to the excellent French railway system, it was a relatively easy journey to Biarritz via Orthez, with just a single change at Bayonne. We luxuriated in the availability of the train's water-closet, which had a proper sit-down toilet, rather than the alarming foot pads and hole-in-ground at BETAP.

We had a wonderful time in Biarritz. Everything was stunning – the weather, the beaches, the food, the wine and especially the local girls. As a result, we got a little too carried away, and when we finally staggered back to the station we discovered that we had missed the last connecting train to Pau. This could spell disaster for our young careers – we could not contemplate getting reported AWOL from a French training camp. Think of the embarrassment.

We decided to hitch-hike to Orthez, in the hope that the first train from there to Pau would arrive in time for morning parade. The next two hours were spent waving, begging and pleading to the passing cars and lorries, but each drove past us without a pause. The evening was getting quite late, and the more we sobered up, the more concerned we got. The situation was starting to look hopeless.

However, our prayers were finally answered, very appropriately, when a Citroen 2CV pulled up, driven by a Roman Catholic priest in full regalia.

I explained our predicament in my best French, and the priest could not have been friendlier.

'*Pas de problème, mes jeunes amis. Je vais à Orthez … allons-y, allons-y!*'

Delighted, we clambered in, with beanpole Robert taking the front seat and the rest of us squashed in the back. After a little polite French chitchat, we dozed off, occasionally disturbed by the 2CV rolling alarmingly as the priest wrestled with steering wheel, gear lever and cassock.

It was some time later that I was woken up by Robert urgently hissing at me from the front seat.

'Charles … CHARLES! … Wake UP!'

'Er … what is it?'

'What should I do?'

'What on earth do you mean?'

'WHAT SHOULD I DO? The priest! He … he's … playing with my willy!'

It was then that I first showed I had the makings of a British Army officer.

'Robert, we have to get to Orthez. For heaven's sake, let him do what he wants!'

We arrived at La Gare d'Orthez just before midnight, albeit with one of us rather less morally and spiritually intact than the others. The station was locked, but we clambered over a fence and caught a few hours' sleep on platform benches until the first morning train took us back to Pau, just in time for morning parade.

* * *

We happened to be in Pau at a very controversial time. The French paratroopers had been mutinying in Algeria, demanding what was called 'L'Algérie Française' i.e. for France to retain control of Algeria rather than grant it independence. They felt very strongly that, given they had been fighting a colonial war in Algeria since 1954, it was only right to retain control.

As a result, President de Gaulle was not popular in the BETAP Officers' Mess. We discovered this on our first Saturday night there.

A large portrait of the President hung in the centre of one wall of the Mess. After dinner, we heard a shouted command from somewhere and all the officers present suddenly turned to face the portrait. A grizzled senior officer, whose name I forget but whose face resembled a crazy-paved patio, collared me and yelled a command which sounded very much to me like 'Turn the President to the wall!' I gave him a startled look, but he just pointed to the portrait and grinned menacingly.

Unknown to us young Brits, we had suddenly become front and centre in a weekly act of sedition, in which the youngest person present in the Mess would be ordered to turn the unpopular President's portrait around to face the wall.

Amid a growing crescendo of cheers and jeers, I nervously wove my way between the tables until I reached the portrait, which was hung by a cord in a solid wooden frame. I grabbed the portrait on one side and dramatically stepped back and to the side so that, as I turned to face the crowd, de Gaulle swung around to face the wall.

There was an almighty roar and thunderous applause, which I naturally assumed was for my bravura performance, until I turned back to the frame to see that I had revealed the most detailed colour portrait of Brigitte Bardot. Stark naked.

* * *

After more torturous days of practice on the training ground, including repeatedly jumping out of a dummy aeroplane, we finally got our first chance to jump for real.

We climbed on board a Nord Noratlas military transport plane, at the end of a line of around thirty French cadets, each of us strapped up with a parachute in front and one behind. I've never been more frightened in all my life.

The plane had climbed to a gut-melting height when suddenly someone was yelling '*Vite! Vite!*' Only then did I realize we had been put at the end of the line for a reason, i.e. we were the first to jump. Everyone behind us in the line started to shuffle forwards and we were slowly pushed towards the back ramp of the plane. There were two instructors at the open doorway, one on each side. They unceremoniously gave each of us a shove, and I found myself spinning through the air, screaming my head off. Thankfully it was not a free-fall jump – my parachute opened due to the static line yanking it, I felt the sudden pull, and then a wonderful floating sensation.

On the way down the instructors, who had jumped with us, were yelling instructions such as 'Left cord!' and 'Feet together!' We all landed safely, feeling rather exhilarated and ready to go again.

*　　*　　*

Unfortunately, that first jump was on a Friday afternoon and there were no more jumps scheduled until next Monday. At least that meant that we had a weekend to amuse ourselves.

On the evening after that first jump, we were asked to parade with the rest of the cadets, but we Brits were told not to wear uniform. We all marched downtown to the middle of Pau, which is a lovely place, to find a huge bonfire in the middle of the town square. All the troops from the training school were there, over 500 of them, but they were all wearing khaki berets instead of the traditional red parachute beret.

I asked a cadet what was going on.

'Well, because of what *Les Paras* have been up to in Algeria, our government has said that we are no longer to wear the red berets again. So tonight, we are going to march through Pau, and when we reach the bonfire we are going to throw our khaki berets into the flames.'

And that is what happened. The atmosphere was extraordinary, with thousands of people watching as the French military all marched through the square. As each one passed the bonfire he defiantly threw his khaki beret into the flames.

The next morning, we were woken up by the Assistant British Military Attaché, who had rushed down from the Embassy.

'Gentlemen – pack everything, we are leaving in ten minutes.'

'Why, Sir?'

This chap was not used to being questioned.

'Because, boy, there is going to be a mutiny in the French Army. Last night here in Pau, they all marched through the middle of the town and burned their berets.'

'But sir, that was just a protest.'

'Listen, boy, when I want your opinion, I will ask for it. You are an Officer Cadet and I am a Lieutenant Colonel – do you understand?'

'Yes, Sir.'

'Now pack immediately, we need to go and see the Commandant.'

We had no option but to pack up, which we did. We were then taken in to see the Commandant, who was a Colonel in the French Army.

'Gentlemen, I am very sorry that you are being taken away prematurely by your Attaché. You have only done one parachute jump. To qualify for your French parachute wings, you must do at least ten jumps. However, each of you is to be presented with a French red parachute beret – with the cap badge – as a souvenir of your time in Pau. Maybe when things get better, you can come back again and complete your training.'

So that was it. We had to get in the car and leave. Of course, there never was another French Revolution, although it was later discovered that it had come closer than anyone had realized, with preparations for a fully planned coup d'état, including paratroopers descending on Paris.

But to this day I have the red beret of *Les Paras*, with the cap badge, in pride of place in my study.

*   *   *

Part of our RMAS officer training was to visit the other services, to get an idea of what the Royal Navy and the RAF got up to. Given the naval history of my mother's family, I was looking forward to our visit to Portsmouth, but the trip took on an extra dimension when I discovered that the officer in charge of our visit was the Captain of the present-day HMS *Murray*, a type-14 class frigate.

I was itching to show off my ancestral link to Admiral George Murray to anyone who would stand still long enough. I finally got my chance in front of the whole cadet group, while we were receiving our final briefing from the rather pompous Captain. When he was finished, he asked if there were any last questions. My hand shot up.

'Sir, I have a question.'

'Yes?

'Sir, I believe the motto of your ship HMS *Murray* is "Murray or None" – is that correct?

'Why, yes, it is.'

'Sir, do you happen to know the origin of that motto?'

The Captain was suddenly rather nonplussed. Flushing crimson, he turned to his second-in-command, who gave an apologetic shrug.

On their confessing that they did not know, I smugly proceeded to give them the story of my ancestor's role as Lord Nelson's Captain of

Fleet. Preparations were being made to set sail for what turned out to be the Battle of Trafalgar, but Admiral George Murray was on leave as his father had recently died and he was organizing the funeral and his estate. Nelson had such a high regard for Murray that, when asked whom he would like to appoint as temporary Captain of Fleet, he replied simply, 'Murray or none.' It therefore transpired that Nelson had no Captain of Fleet at the battle of Trafalgar. The role was unofficially picked up by Thomas Hardy, who was Nelson's Flag Captain and famously was with him when he died.

The Captain and his second-in-command thanked me for enlightening them, but they were clearly none too pleased at the Royal Navy being shown up by a snotty young Army officer cadet. My colleagues were all delighted, however, so I didn't pay for any drinks for a week.

*   *   *

All 1,200 officer cadets at Sandhurst were on parade. It was the day before the passing-out of my intake. We all needed to practise our square-bashing so that we wouldn't trip up over each other in front of Her Majesty.

Regimental Sergeant Major (RSM) J.C. Lord, a war hero and a quite terrifying man, stepped forward and brought us all to attention with his commanding bellow.

'SAN'URST! San'urst ... SHUN!'

The parade smartly came to attention. The RSM then frowned.

'Sergeant Major, Waterloo Company!'

'Sir!'

'There's an officer cadet – rear rank, second from left – he's being idle!'

'Got him, Sir – that's Officer Cadet Lyons.'

The RSM shouted to the culprit.

'Officer Cadet Lyons!'

Terry Lyons woke from his reverie with a start.

'Sir?'

'I know you – you're one of the 'orrible ones!'

'Ah ... could you qualify that, please, Sir?'

Giggling broke out in the ranks. The RSM turned purple.

'What do you mean, *qualify*?! Go and apologize to Queen Victoria at once!'

Apologizing to Queen Victoria was a common punishment handed out to any unfortunate cadet who had caught the eye for the wrong reason. On receiving the order, the cadet would have to raise his rifle above his head, run all the way down King's Walk to the statue of Queen Victoria which stood at the end of the Walk, run around the statue and then run all the way back to his position on parade.

Terry Lyons duly raised his rifle above his head and trotted off towards the statue. However, when he got there, he stopped, saluted, presented arms and stood to attention, seemingly in earnest conversation. He then shouldered arms and sauntered off, instead of returning to the parade.

He later regaled us with what had happened when he was tracked down and marched in to the RSM's office.

'Officer Cadet Lyons – explain yourself!'

'Well, you see, Sir, on receiving the order to go and apologize to Queen Victoria, I ran down the King's Walk and stopped to make my apology.'

'And … ?'

'Well, I explained to Her Majesty that I had just been to my sister's twenty-first birthday party last night and had only got to my bed at 4.00am and so was very, very tired. Queen Victoria said she perfectly understood and that she liked a good party herself, so she gave me the rest of the day off.'

Officer Cadet Lyons was kept under close arrest overnight, but thankfully was released the next morning with dire warnings about the consequences should he misbehave in any way whatsoever. He duly passed out with the rest of us and was commissioned into the Royal Artillery.

Three Royal Scots were commissioned on that same day. My two close friends, Patrick Cardwell-Moore and Robert Watson, passed out with good grades and flying colours. I scraped through as the junior of the three. Many, many years later, Patrick retired as a Lieutenant Colonel, Robert as a Colonel, and eventually I as a Brigadier. Two hares and a tortoise.

Chapter 3

Be Not Afraid of Grittiness

I was delighted to hear that my first tour of duty as a newly commissioned 2nd Lieutenant was to be to 'Italian Libya', as it had been known. I still retained some of my childhood command of the wonderful language from our time in Trieste. Despite Italy having surrendered their Libyan colony after the Second World War, I imagined that the posting would be like returning to a much-loved Italian way of life for a while, albeit with less pasta and more sand.

I was stationed in the ex-Italian Army Medenine Barracks, as part of the British Army garrison in Tripoli. It was not a demanding posting, given that sixteen years had passed since the end of the war that had led to the creation of such garrisons.

Italian influence in Libya goes back to Roman times, and the country came under Italian rule again following a war with the Ottoman Empire for the territory in 1911–12. I mention this war because what I didn't appreciate as a young officer in 1962 was its global significance – the weakness shown against Italy by the Turkish Ottoman empire encouraged the rise of Balkan nationalism against their Ottoman 'oppressors', directly leading to the Balkan wars of 1912 and 1913 and hence to the assassination of Archduke Ferdinand in 1914 – 'the shot that was heard around the world'.

Following the Great War, Italy implemented quite brutal tactics in Libya to suppress local nationalists and encouraged tens of thousands of Italians, mostly farmers, to move to Libya and settle there. When the Second World War broke out, a Libyan army was raised to fight with the Allies in the hope of bringing the Italian occupation to an end.

Thus, contrary to my naive expectations, I arrived in Libya in 1962 to find a country where the many Italians who had moved there during original Italian colonization, or had been born there, were barely tolerated or evenly openly abused.

* * *

One of our regular pastimes in Tripoli was to visit the local US Air Force at Wheelus Air Base. It was the largest American military facility outside of the USA and had everything, from its own beach to a bowling alley. It was all great fun – out of town, totally safe, great food and very cheap.

However, the Commander of the base was a prude. Entertainers were regularly flown in from Germany on USAAF planes, but most of their shows, particularly the more risqué cabarets, were banned from the Officers' Club by the Commander and were only performed, in a limited fashion, for the other ranks.

One day, I received a special plea from some of our American pals to engage my acting skills. A rather spectacular all-girl cabaret act had arrived and was due to perform at the airbase – but not for the officers, as per the Commander's standing instructions. I was asked to meet the girls, who were spending some time on the beach during the day, with the aim of convincing them that they had been given permission to perform their full floor show performance at the Officers' Club that evening.

I duly met the girls at the beach and introduced myself in my best Midwest American accent as Major Rougecou of the USAAF, committee member of the Wheelus Air Base Officers' Club. I had a lovely chat with them, during which I learned something about their act and gave them the good news that they had permission to perform their full floor show that night.

Word soon spread of the spectacular act lined up for that evening. The Officers' Club was packed to the rafters with officers and guests, including a sizeable number of us British, although I had to keep a low profile in case one of the girls recognized me. After a terrific meal, the stage was set and, to the backdrop of a live band, we were treated to the most eye-wateringly entertaining strip-show.

But news and raunchy music travel fast and, midway through the act, the Commander stormed into the Club and clambered on to the stage, in a misguided attempt to have the performance stopped. Many of the audience didn't recognize him, assumed he was part of the entertainment and gamely barracked and jeered him off the stage to allow the show to continue.

The next day, the furious Commander organized an investigation into what had happened. The girls were interviewed and insisted that they had been given permission for the show by one of the Commander's own officers. Despite a major witch-hunt across Wheelus Air Base, the handsome and charming Major Rougecou was obviously never tracked down.

*   *   *

One Saturday morning, not long after I had arrived in Tripoli, I took a stroll to the local market and bought a very large bunch of grapes, which I proceeded to eat while distractedly enjoying a leisurely walk in the glorious sunshine.

The next day I felt very, *very* ill. All the other officers had either gone to church, or the beach, or away for the day. I was on my own in my room, moaning and groaning and feeling awful.

Captain Roger Swinfen (later Lord Swinfen) and his girlfriend Patricia Anne happened to pass by. Patricia was a nurse at the British Military Hospital in Tripoli, and as they walked along the corridor past my room, she heard my groans and came striding in.

'Charles – you sound terrible.'

'I am – I think I'm dying.'

Bless her. She took one look at me and called for an ambulance, which came from the nearby Military Hospital. I was put on a stretcher and immediately taken off to the emergency ward, where they did various things to me that I cannot or do not want to remember. The Commanding Officer came to see me, and then the Brigadier came to see me. I recall dizzily thinking it was as though they were coming to say their goodbyes.

It turned out that I was suffering from a form of cyanide poisoning. In those days, some local Italian farmers sprayed their grapes with hydrogen cyanide as a pesticide. Unnoticed by me, there were signs around the market telling you to wash the grapes thoroughly before eating. I didn't see the signs, and I hadn't washed my grapes.

Fortunately, the local medics were well prepared for such emergencies, as I was not the first Brit to have succumbed following Bacchanalian over-consumption. They treated me with some ready-to-hand doses of amyl nitrate, which I understand these days is apparently a trendy recreational drug called 'poppers'. I was always ahead of my time.

The medics told me later that my reaction to the poison had been surprisingly extreme. Apparently, if Patricia had not happened to pass my room, I would probably have died – not from heroically charging an enemy position under intense crossfire, but from greedily munching a very large bunch of grapes without rinsing them first.

*   *   *

While based in Medenine Barracks, junior 2nd lieutenant officers did not have a room to themselves. We shared a room, and there was a communal bathroom that everyone used. My good friend Robert Watson was my roommate. We each simply had a bed, a chest-of-drawers and a cupboard.

However, in those days you also had a batman, known as a 'soldier servant'. He was in your platoon, he was your bodyguard and he would look after you. Every morning, he would wake you up, give you a cup of tea and lay out for you the uniform you had to wear that day – he knew what was on the agenda, you didn't. You simply put on the uniform your batman provided.

One morning, prior to a big parade, someone rushed into our room while we were both still asleep.

'What are you two playing at? You are on parade in fifteen minutes!'

'Really? Oh, yes, so we are – hell, where are our uniforms?'

It turned out that our two batmen, Private Ware and Private Scott, had been fighting the night before in the NAAFI, arguing about us, of all things. Batmen took their roles very seriously.

'Ah always turn oot ma officer better'n you!'

'Ach awa' wi' ya, man! Ma officer is way better dressed th'n yours!'

'Naw he bloody well isnae! Ha' you seen the quality o' ma officer's clothes, his dinner jaicket …'

They proceeded to have the mother of all fights and were arrested by the Regimental Police. As a result, they spent the night in jail and were not at liberty in the morning to wake us up with a cup of tea and lay out our uniforms.

The following day, they appeared as part of what was called 'Commanding Officer's Orders', charged with being drunk and fighting. They were marched in and ordered to give their explanation. The result was not that they were sent for a week in jail as they expected. Instead, they were fined a week's wages each, which was far more painful.

Robert and I were then sent for by the Adjutant.

'Now, chaps, your two batmen have just been fined a week's wages. It turns out they were each standing up for their officer, i.e. you pair – God knows why. I suggest the weekly tip from each of you needs to be rather larger than usual.'

At the end of the week, as instructed, I discreetly reimbursed my loyal batman, as did Robert.

*   *   *

We were on a firing exercise in the desert, south of Tripoli. Nothing but sand and rock as far as the eye could see.

The battalion second-in-command, Major Joe McCance, was leading us. The wonderful McCance clan had several generations who served in The Royal Scots.

'Right, gentlemen – some live firing now. We'll use mortars, anti-tank guns, and machine guns. See those rocks and mounds way over there? That's our target. Bearing – 116 degrees.'

'Sir!'

'Range – 1,000 yards,'

'Sir!'

'Stand by – FIRE!'

Everybody loosed off with our mortars, artillery and machine guns at the specified area of mounds and rocks.

'Cease fire! CEASE FIRE!'

As the dust cleared, we looked through our binoculars and were astonished to see a group of people emerging from the ground amid rocks we had been firing at. These people turned out to be troglodytes – people who lived in cave dwellings dug into the earth. We'd given them a hell of a shaking, although thankfully we did not injure anyone.

We got the local police involved and explained that we had been told we could go out into the desert for our live firing exercises, but we had certainly not been told that there were people *living* out there in these cave holes. Nevertheless, it was not a good move and unfortunately made the British even more unpopular with the locals.

*   *   *

The sport of boxing is greatly encouraged in the Army. Major McCance was ex-SAS and a great boxing man. He always organized the annual battalion boxing competition, for which he decreed that all officers had to enter, irrespective of skill level.

The Major brought in Quartermaster Sergeant Instructor Terry Holmes from the Royal Army Physical Training Corps to take all officers for extra training to improve their boxing skills. I had only boxed once, at Sandhurst, and got a broken nose for my trouble. That was actually the second time it had been broken, after suffering a skiing accident as a child. As a result, the medic gave me a pass from any further boxing, for fear my weak nose would crumble completely.

My role at the battalion boxing event was therefore reduced to acting as 'second' to my roommate Robert Watson who, despite being no better a boxer, had failed to come up with an excuse to wriggle out of Major McCance's decree. What was worse for Robert was that B Company was very short of boxers who could enter the heavier weight classes. He discovered this when his Sergeant Major was finalizing the entries.

'Now, Sir, I believe you are a light-heavyweight, yes?'

'No, Sergeant-Major, I am a light-middleweight.'

'Are you sure, Sir? I could ask the Company Commander ...'

'Oh, all right, Sergeant Major – I'll be light-heavyweight.'

Robert was not happy. Not only was he not a boxer, but now he would be up against opponents who could be more than 20lbs heavier than him. My suggestion that he could presumably run faster did not help.

The boxing tournament turned out to be full of surprises, however.

There had only been five entries into the light-heavyweight division, and the draw had put Robert into a preliminary bout, the winner of which would join the remaining three in the semi-finals. To everyone's surprise, Robert won this preliminary bout with a knockout. I was impressed, although Robert still insists to this day that the young Jock he was up against simply fell on the floor for a ten-count as soon as Robert waved a glove at him.

This unexpected win propelled him into a semi-final against a real big ruffian from A Company. As luck would have it, however, said ruffian was a no-show on the night, having been put on a charge for starting a scuffle the previous day. With that bout declared a 'walkover', Robert was now in the Battalion light-heavyweight boxing final and, as chance would have it, he was up against the other light-heavyweight entry from his own B Company – Private Scott, his own batman.

We all knew that Scott was a good boxer. He had been the bouncer at an infamous bar in Edinburgh before joining up, so he knew how to handle himself. Rank means nothing in the Army when you step inside the boxing ring, but it was also obvious from the first bell that the close relationship between officer and batman meant even less.

I watched between the gaps in my fingers as my friend got an absolute pasting from his batman for three minutes solid. Major McCance was not impressed with this one-sided final and glared with increasing anger at Robert's hapless attempts to defend himself from the onslaught.

Somehow, Robert managed to stay upright for the whole of the first round. Even more surprisingly, he bravely staggered out to re-engage the enemy at the start of the second. He told me afterwards he was more scared of the Major than of Private Scott.

More punishment was duly delivered, only interrupted for a few seconds at a time while Robert picked himself up off the canvas. He was hanging on grimly as the bell was about to sound to give him some respite, when a crunching 'haymaker' from his batman floored him again. The bell rang before the ten-count could be completed but, as I helped Robert back to our corner, I knew the contest was over.

The referee came over to check if Robert was able to continue, but before he could make a decision, the towel was thrown in – by Private Scott's corner. The young lad had managed to break his thumb with that last punch and had to retire from the contest, leaving Robert with bragging rights for the rest of his career as a Battalion light-heavyweight boxing champion, and the only man in the British Army to have TKO'd the opposition with his chin.

*   *   *

I was on duty one Sunday when I received a telephone call from an American at the Oasis Oil Company's drilling site about 200 miles south of Tripoli.

'Say, are you the Duty Officer of the Scottish Regiment?'

'Yes, Sir – this is 2nd Lieutenant Ritchie of The Royal Scots.'

'We've a problem here and I hope you guys can help. We had one hell of a *ghibli* here last night, and it's uncovered a couple of army lorries with two bodies inside ...'

A violent desert storm, known as a *ghibli*, had shifted the sand dunes and uncovered two German trucks from the war, with the bodies of their unfortunate drivers still in the cabs.

I was ordered to travel with two coffins and a team of soldiers and engineers to recover the bodies. We set off in the morning into the desert on the main road south. Sure enough, just about half a mile from the drill site, we spotted the two lorries. It was quite an astonishing sight. They had been about 90 per cent uncovered by the storm and looked in perfect condition; the poor drivers in the cabs looked as if they were simply asleep at the wheel, despite having been dead for more than twenty years.

Our guess was that they had perished in the same sort of major sandstorm that had just uncovered them. You can't drive in a sandstorm because you can't see where you are going, so they had probably stopped to try to wait it out.

We removed the bodies and placed them in the coffins. We then inspected the contents of the lorries to check for dangerous explosives and the like. However, we found nothing more than case upon case of tinned food, which we removed. Our engineers had various bits of equipment with them, including some batteries, so out of curiosity they connected these up to the lorries and tried to fire up the engines – and lo and behold, both started first time. German engineering! However, it was impossible to shift the vehicles, so we simply left them there.

On our return to Tripoli, the coffins were handed over to the German Consul to deal with. The cases of food were also taken away, but not before we had checked them out and found the tins of peas, stew, etc. to be perfectly edible.

*   *   *

I was a decent swimmer as a young man. I became the battalion's swimming officer while in Tripoli, responsible for ensuring all the men could swim and giving lessons where necessary.

In the autumn of 1962, it was our turn to host the annual Middle East Swimming Championships, which over the preceding years had become quite a big event, with competitors flying in from various British Armed Forces stationed all across the Mediterranean and Middle East.

I got heavily involved in the planning of this major event and was looking forward to it immensely. I was therefore not at all happy that the USA and Russia selfishly decided to have their Cuban Missile Crisis just days before our Swimming Gala was due to kick off.

As the world waited nervously for news, fearful of what fate might befall the human race, military services across the globe urgently dusted off their nuclear contingency plans and held crisis meetings. The Royal Scots in Libya were no different – the Brigade Commander held an emergency meeting in his office.

'Charles – damn this Cuban nonsense – all military flights have been cancelled. Which teams can still make it to our Swimming Championships?'

'Just ourselves, plus the RAF boys at Idris, Sir.'

'Bugger it – we'll go ahead anyway.'

So we went ahead and held our Swimming Championships. There were not enough competitors to hold every race, and heats were not required, but to my mind the backstroke event was a particular highlight as it was won convincingly by yours truly.

I proudly stepped up to receive my trophy from the Brigadier, but he soon burst my bubble.

'Well done, Ritchie – Middle East Backstroke Champion.'

'Thank you, Sir.'

'Don't get too excited – your winning time is the slowest ever recorded.'

*   *   *

Our Adjutant, Captain David Hay, was a very well-spoken chap from the very select Morningside area of Edinburgh. While in Tripoli he had 'adopted' a dachshund ,which he called Tom. Contrary to regulations, he kept Tom in the drawing room of his Field Officer's suite, right next to the Mess.

A few weeks previously, a stray dog had caused a lot of trouble, barking incessantly and eventually biting someone. Captain Hay had ordered me to dispatch and bury the stray – an order which, under protest, I eventually complied with behind the Mess building.

One night thereafter, I decided to teach Captain Hay a lesson. I got on to the roof of the Mess building and lowered a sausage on a string down the chimney into the Captain's drawing room. Little Tom went mad yapping and trying to find this sausage, barking his head off. Captain Hay proceeded to yell at Tom from his bedroom next door to shut up, but to no avail. After a good five minutes of this I removed the sausage, went around to the back of the Mess building and started digging another dog-sized grave.

This gave Tom enough time to calm down, and the Captain enough time to fall asleep. I then crept into his drawing room and removed little Tom, who finally got to eat his sausage while hidden away in one of my colleagues' bedrooms. I then went to the back of the Mess building with my shotgun and fired a shot into the air.

The Captain quickly emerged from his bedroom.

'What the hell was that shot?'

My colleagues were ready.

'Ah, Sir, we wondered where you had been. That dachshund has been barking for ages and keeping us all awake, so Charles Ritchie has done what we know you want done in these circumstances with nuisance dogs – he's shot it.'

Poor Captain Hay ran to the back of the Mess building to find me standing with my gun next to a fresh grave. Before he could react, Tom was released and trotted happily up to his master. I hoped the Captain would see the funny side, but his sense of humour went AWOL. We never did get on terribly well after that.

* * *

There was no mains water supply in the barracks, so we maintained a number of large makeshift pools dotted around the place in case of fire, which was an ever-present danger. I was the Fire Officer, and we practised once a week with a petrol-powered water pump which we would push up to one of the pools, drop the hose in and start the pump.

After many weeks of dutiful practice, the great day came when there was a real emergency. The Orderly Room caught fire somehow, with all the paperwork in it, and part of the Quartermaster's Stores next door. The alarm was raised, and my fire team and I rushed to our mobile pump, pushed it to the pond nearest to the Orderly Room and threw the sucker end of the hose into the water.

Normally, in practice runs, one of the men started the pump. However, in the circumstances, I thought it best to show leadership and so I urgently proceeded to try to start it myself. But try as I might, pulling on the starting cord for all my worth, it would not start – it spluttered and coughed briefly, but refused to cooperate.

With the fire quickly taking hold, we resorted to buckets and human chains. This eventually succeeded in controlling the fire, although the damage done was much greater than if we had had a working pump.

Fortunately, there were no injuries. The Quartermaster somehow managed to exaggerate the losses so he was delighted to get surplus stores in replacement, and the Orderly Sergeant joked that there were certain files he had wanted destroyed, so he had taken the opportunity to run around various offices to collect fuel for the fire.

After the dust had settled, the team tried the pump again. It started first time. In my haste and panic, I had failed to turn on the fuel switch. Oops.

I was promptly and permanently relieved of my duties as Fire Officer.

*　*　*

Bob Filler, a USAAF pilot stationed at Wheelus Air Base, became a great friend during my time in Libya. I happened to mention to him one day that I was helping to prepare for a major parade at Medenine Barracks to commemorate Her Majesty the Queen's Birthday.

On the morning of the parade, I received a phone call from Bob.

'Hey, Charlie – good luck with your parade today for the Queen.'

'Er … thanks, Bob.'

'What time is the big salute and all that?'

'1100 hours.'

'Okay-dokey.'

Strange conversation, I thought … but soon forgot it, as I returned to my last-minute preparations.

The parade duly went ahead, with 600 British Army troops doing their best square-bashing in front of the General. Just as everyone lined up for the main salute there was an almighty roar as a USAAF F100 Super

Sabre jet fighter flew at tree-top height across the parade ground, right over our heads. The noise was painful, and a dust storm whipped up around us, through which we could just see the jet climb and perform a spectacular barrel roll before disappearing over the horizon.

There was an impromptu investigation into how the USAAF had managed to gatecrash our parade in such disruptive fashion, and I had to confess that it was Bob Filler who had performed the fly-past. Thinking on my feet, I claimed it was an officially sanctioned gesture from our USAAF allies at Wheelus airbase as a special honour to Her Majesty the Queen, which somehow managed to get us both out of any further trouble.

*   *   *

I discovered a quite startling remnant of the Italian colonization of Libya while on a day's R&R with my good friend and colleague, Patrick Cardwell-Moore.

We had come across an old map of Tripolitania in the barracks' map store, dating back to long before the last war and showing the existence of an Italian settlement just off the main road between Tripoli in the west and Tarhuna in the south. Patrick and I decided to take a drive out in the trusty Volkswagen Beetle that we had clubbed together to buy, to see if this village was still in existence.

We drove out along the main road south of Tripoli until the map showed the settlement to be a mile or so to the west, so we took a side road in that direction. After a mile or more, there was still no sign of any town or village anywhere. We were about to give up and consign this old map to the bin, when we saw what I can only describe as a camouflaged gate at the side of the road. On closer inspection, we found it was a huge iron structure with bits of trees deliberately stuck in it, obviously intended to blend in with the strips of foliage on either side of the road.

We opened the gate, drove through, closed the gate behind us and proceeded along a tiny single-track road until, over the brow of a hill, we suddenly came across it – a sizeable village, complete with a church, cafés and shops. Around on the surrounding hillsides were well-tended farms with vineyards, orchards and the like.

Intrigued, we slowly drove into the main village square, where we were delighted to see a bar, although the locals sitting at tables were open-mouthed at the sight of a British-registered vehicle appearing in the middle of their well-hidden settlement.

We parked the car and walked into the bar, to be met by a rather menacing silence. There was a huge portrait behind the bar of none other than Mussolini. Realizing this could be a sticky situation, I fell back on my schoolboy Italian, through which I managed to explain the facts behind our innocent visit and insisted that Patrick and I were actually great admirers of Mussolini, despite his choice of friends.

The locals were very keen to hear how we had found them and warmed to us over the sharing of several bottles of amazing village wine. They explained that the area had been established as an Italian settlement in the years before the last war and how everyone was very keen to stay in their little idyll, hopefully untouched and untroubled by the political situation around them.

With repeated assurances that their secret was safe with us, we were escorted back down the track and through the camouflaged gate. I remember looking back to see a couple of them diligently sweeping away any evidence of our sandy tyre tracks on the road from the gateway.

As we drove rather tipsily back to Tripoli, I romantically imagined our Italian Brigadoon village disappearing into the evening mist, perhaps to appear again in 100 years' time.

Chapter 4

Now is the Winter of our Dismal Tent

I arrived back in the UK from Libya in January 1963 and was posted to Tidworth in Wiltshire, where I was to be based while attending the Small Arms School in Hythe in Kent, followed by the School of Infantry in Warminster.

I no longer had a half-share in the Volkswagen Beetle, which had been left in Tripoli with Patrick. After much debate, we had decided who should keep the car by the dramatic method of a coin-toss, surrounded by our amused colleagues. Obviously, I lost.

Needing some wheels, I promptly bought a little second-hand mini-van. I was told in no uncertain terms by my superiors that my little mini-van 'is in no way an officer's vehicle', but it was all I could afford and it was roomy in the back which, for a young bachelor, had its advantages.

* * *

We had a good mix of chaps while at Hythe, all from different regiments, and spent many a raucous evening in the local hostelries or at some party or another.

One particular rascal was Mike Ogilvie of The Black Watch, who was part of the Demonstration Battalion at Warminster and so had access to all sorts of pyrotechnics. One night, on getting back to barracks from a particularly rowdy party, around thirty of us decided it would be fun to use some plastic explosive to wake up Nigel Chamberlain, a young officer from the Guards who had decided not to party with us.

Mike appeared with a stick of plastic explosive, so we lit a one-minute fuse outside Nigel's door and then, in traditional fashion, knocked loudly and ran off giggling. Nigel took what seemed like an age to stumble out of bed and open his door, saw the fizzing stick at his feet with a rapidly-shortening fuse, yelled a profanity and slammed the door shut. Seconds later, the explosive went up, the door blew in, the windows blew out, and the ceiling came down.

Fortunately, Nigel was uninjured, having taken the sensible precaution of diving under his bed. However, the next day, we all had to parade in front of the Camp Commandant, who gave us an imperial bollocking. He was riled, but clearly hadn't been to see the damage for himself, as he rabbited on about how this was a lesson for us on 'the dangers of using a thunderflash indoors'.

We couldn't contain our laughter at this point – goodness knows what he would have said if he had known it was plastic explosive we had used. Unfortunately, our giggling riled him further.

'Right, you lot, enough is enough. You will all pay in full for the repairs required – and you will parade at 0630 tomorrow for a double session on the assault course.'

This was severe punishment indeed. The assault course was a beast which was best avoided at all costs. We got together and decided something had to be done. Late that evening, armed with saws and axes, we scurried off down to the assault course and spent half the night dismantling the whole thing.

The next morning, we dutifully gathered for parade and were marched down to the assault course, where we loudly expressed our disappointment that there seemed to be nothing there for us to enjoy.

It was good fun at the time, but we had to pay the bills, not just for the barracks repairs but also for the complete rebuild of an assault course, which put a severe dampener on our partying funds for a long time afterwards.

*　*　*

While back at Tidworth, a wonderful Royal Scot officer by the name of Robin Keyes got married. The wedding was held somewhere up the M1, which in those days was still very new. I had never driven on a motorway before, but I successfully drove to the wedding from Tidworth with another officer.

It was a wonderful day and all the guests had a fantastic time. Unfortunately, it was only at the end of the evening that it dawned on us that, rather stupidly, we had not planned anywhere to stay for the night.

I'm ashamed to say that in those days drinking and driving was very commonplace. I simply agreed with my colleague that we might as well drive back to Tidworth.

On our way back we quickly realized we needed what is known as a 'comfort break', so I turned off the motorway. There were not many roadside service stations in those early days, but eventually we stopped at a café that was still open. As I say, I had never been on a motorway before, and when we set off again I simply used my excellent sense of direction to rejoin the motorway to head home.

It was now late at night, and as we pootled down the road there was no other traffic to be seen. After a few minutes, I noticed to my left through a hedgerow that there was a vehicle also heading south on a parallel road. Before I could work out what road that could be, I saw the lights of a car coming directly towards me, dangerously overtaking another. He angrily flashed his lights at me, and I at him – we just managed to avoid each other – and it was only then that I realized that I was travelling south in the fast lane of the north-bound carriageway of the M1.

Fortunately for me, in those days there were no crash-barriers in the central reservation. At a gap in the hedge I simply drove the car over the grass bank and across the central reservation and joined the traffic heading south on the correct carriageway. My passenger didn't even wake from his drunken slumber.

*   *   *

From Hythe we moved to Warminster for the Platoon Commander's course, the highlight of which was a two-day defence exercise on Salisbury Plain.

One key element of this was the need to dig various trenches, including a shelter trench for our sleeping accommodation. I was friendly with one of the officers in the 5th Royal Inniskilling Dragoon Guards, who were stationed at Warminster to provide the 'enemy' for the training exercise. He kindly tipped me off as to exactly where my platoon was going to be told to dig our trenches.

Armed with this key info, my trench-mate and I went out the evening before the exercise was due to begin, armed with a variety of household furnishings which we hid in the bushes nearby.

The next day, loaded with our large packs, we were marched out to our location on Salisbury Plain and ordered to dig our trenches in exactly the spot my informant had indicated. When we were finished, our trench had matching carpet and curtains, some pictures, a small table and a battery-powered reading lamp. It looked absolutely marvellous.

Our Australian instructor duly arrived to inspect our trench work, but instead of the usual arrangement of a groundsheet and a couple of sleeping bags, he found our luxurious little room.

'Ritchie! How the bloody hell have you managed this?'

'Sir, it's amazing what you can fit in a large pack these days.'

The Chief Instructor was called for, who thankfully found the whole thing quite amusing.

'Ritchie – I'm guessing you managed to find out where you were due to dig in?'

'I can't lie, Sir – yes, that's correct'.

'Good piece of initiative. Carry on.'

*   *   *

Another training week while at Warminster was for 'Armoured Infantry', which involved learning how to deploy Armoured Personnel Carriers (APCs). Unfortunately, during a night exercise, Gordon Batty's APC got completely lost and ended up in Larkhill, driving around the Royal Artillery's steeplechase course.

On inspecting his route the next day, it was clear that Gordon and his driver had done quite a demolition job on the steeplechase course. He did argue, rather reasonably, that the course is located on Salisbury Plain and does look like open terrain with just the odd hedge or bush.

Despite our best horticultural repair efforts, the Royal Artillery's next weekend meet had to be cancelled. As for Gordon, he had been on an official exercise at the time, so there was no serious punishment other than scoring a rare 'E' grade for the exercise.

*   *   *

An 'E' grade was also handed out during the 'House Clearing' exercise, in which we had to work our way through a mock-up village, clearing each building by chucking a thunderflash in through a window to startle any occupants, before moving in as quickly as possible.

The unfortunate this time was Adrian Mallock, who got a little over-excited with his thunderflash at the start of the exercise. He ran headlong up to the first window, threw the thunderflash in and then immediately dived in after it. There was a loud curse as he realized what he had done, followed by the bang of the thunderflash.

Fortunately, Adrian had had the presence of mind to drop to the ground and stick his fingers in his ears, which avoided any lasting damage other than to his pride. I believe he got an 'A' grade for enthusiasm.

*   *   *

One of the more exciting training courses I attended was at RAF Chivenor, where I trained as a Forward Air Controller (FAC). The role of an FAC was to be in an advanced position, communicating with and directing our fighter aircraft, which would zoom overhead to fire rocket and cannon on enemy positions.

The RAF's main jet fighter at the time was the Hawker Hunter, which at one point held the world air-speed record for fighter aircraft, at over 700 mph. Learning how to direct these jets to a ground target was therefore quite a challenge, although the training did involve actually getting to take the controls of a Hunter while in the air, in order to get a sense of what a fighter pilot would be experiencing while an excitable young Army officer babbled over the radio to him.

It was great fun being trained, although I imagined it would be quite a hairy job and one I never thought for a moment that I would ever be doing for real. Grade 'E' for foresight, Ritchie.

*   *   *

General Aloia, the Italian Chief of the Defence Staff, came to Tidworth for a demonstration of a helicopter assault using our smart new Westland Scout light attack helicopters.

No doubt the good people at Westland were hoping the Italians would buy a few, and the Army Air Corps were keen to show off their new toys, so a rather spectacular demonstration was planned, in which two Hunter fighter jets would soften up the 'enemy' position on the much-abused Sidbury Hill, before our brave boys would be carried into battle by the Scout helicopters to take the hill.

Given the immense potential for cock-up, a dress rehearsal was required. Of course, any mention of a dress rehearsal and I'm at the front of the line. In this case, however, I had to demonstrate my newly-acquired skill as an FAC to orchestrate the two Hunter jets, although that needed no more than the coordinates for Sidbury Hill and the time of their strike – 1448 hours precisely. I would then need to guide in the helicopters. Each Scout was only designed to carry four men in addition to the pilot, and the assault called for 40 men and two 3-inch mortars to lift, so we would need ten helicopters.

More challenging was the need to converse with the General, who didn't speak English. Several years had elapsed since I last spoke Italian, so I was rather apprehensive as to how I would manage in my sketchy Triestino dialect.

On the morning of the dress rehearsal, only two helicopters showed up. We decided we would simply do a reconnaissance flight, so I duly got in the front seat of one of the machines, next to the pilot. Three soldiers squeezed on the bench seat behind us, and we took off towards the planned assault landing point. It was a misty morning and visibility was shockingly poor, so I quickly became quite nervous about how low the pilot was flying and felt obliged to yell something:

'Excuse me, Sir, but I think we are dangerously close to Sidbury Hill.'

The pilot duly yelled back, 'When I want your advice, young man, I'll ask for it.'

At that moment, the mist cleared and we suddenly saw the side of Sidbury Hill right in front of us, less than 50 yards away. The pilot hauled on his controls to bring the nose of the helicopter up, whereupon the landing rails slammed into the side of the hill. Fortunately, the rotor blades smashed against large rocks to one side of us and immediately disintegrated, preventing the helicopter from spinning upside down. As it was, we were all able to unstrap and walk away from the wreck, bruised and shocked but otherwise unhurt.

Despite this minor hiccup, the demonstration went ahead as planned the next day. Rumour had it that every available Scout helicopter in the country had been rounded up. We had a grand total of eight available –

not quite the ten we asked for, but we had already destroyed one so we didn't complain.

The Generalissimo was due to arrive at 1400 but, impatient with the boring British postprandial conversation, he left his lunch appointment early and arrived with us 15 minutes ahead of schedule. Mild panic ensued, accompanied by urgently whispered commands of 'Ritchie, stall him!'

After being introduced to Major Cullins of the Army Air Corps and my esteemed Company Commander Major Addison, the Generalissimo advanced on me, accompanied by his two Italian aides and various British top brass. The introductions took place, whereupon I had the bright idea of engaging our guest in conversation using my rusty Italian. This worked for a few minutes and delighted the General, who thereafter kept up a constant stream of salutes in my direction.

My delaying tactics continued with demonstrations of how to fit four people in the Scout, what the British webbing looked like, our lovely SLR (Self Loading Rifle) and the wonderful autumnal colour of the Salisbury Plain trees.

I then had the bright idea of giving him a demonstration of the new L7 GPMG (General Purpose Machine Gun). He wasn't particularly impressed with the suggestion.

'We have the same in Italy.'

'I know you do, General, but this is different. FIRE!'

After being covered in smoke and dust, he smiled enigmatically, there was a final flurry of salutes and he left to watch the spectacle.

The command was given, and the assault began with pre-arranged artillery cover to soften up the imaginary enemy before the troops arrived. Rather than risking a dodgy shell landing among our guests or, worse still, taking out another of our precious helicopters, we had arranged for the Royal Engineers to set some explosives on the hillside to simulate the artillery barrage. They duly triggered their explosives, which took away half the hillside and several ear drums.

The eight helicopters then flew in, the assault went without a hiccup, the remains of the phantom enemy were driven out, and our brave boys waved their flag from the top of what was left of the beleaguered hill.

Unfortunately, it was now only 1447 hours. Just as the muted applause from the gathered dignitaries subsided, two Hawker Hunters screamed overhead and delivered their simulated opening attacks on the enemy.

Our victorious troops dived for cover just in case, their flag blew away in the wind and all the British top brass held their heads in their hands.

I turned to our guest and smiled.

'A celebratory fly-past for you, General.'

* * *

In January 1964, our company flew to Fort Churchill, Manitoba, to do the one-month Canadian Army Arctic Warfare course. We had lovely heated accommodation, but when camping out on exercise overnight I have never been so cold in all my life.

We also had an unusual problem on the firing range which caused considerable embarrassment to the British Army. Our new rifle, the SLR, was semi-automatic, so that when you fired, the empty cartridge ejected and the recoil pushed the next round from the magazine into the breech. When the first chap fired a round at the range in Fort Churchill, his gun exploded, because the grease in the butt of the rifle which housed the recoil mechanism had frozen rock-solid. Murphy's first law of combat – your weapon is always manufactured by the lowest bidder.

Reports were written, phone calls were made and the British Army for the first time realized that none of their rifles would work in Arctic temperatures. For the remainder of our course, the Canadians very kindly lent each 10-man tent a single old Second World War .303 bolt-action rifle. We were all sworn to secrecy to avoid embarrassing anyone.

* * *

For a bit of fun, I had brought from home a couple of LP records by a popular new band called The Beatles, who had come to prominence less than a year before. The Officers' Mess in Fort Churchill was a rather splendid building, with a lovely large dance floor. At this amazing place they held a terrific party for us, and lots of young Canadian ladies came. I offered our hosts my two LPs to play and everybody went absolutely mad for them – 'This is the best thing we've ever heard.'

At the end of the evening one of the Canadian officers approached me eagerly.

'Charles, we love your Beatles records – will you sell them to us and buy two more when you get back to England?

'What a good idea!'

We quickly organized a little auction and I got more than ten times the purchase price for each. Regretfully, however, I never received the letter of thanks from the Fab Four for having single-handedly established their popularity in Canada.

*   *   *

Part of our training involved camping out in the frozen wilderness, in a 10-man tent holding myself, a sergeant, and eight men. In these conditions you are taught to dig a trench in the snow and ice, through which you crawl into and out of the tent, in order to avoid the tent losing heat. However, we were also warned that the timber wolf population in the area had got rather out of hand. We therefore all took one-hour shifts, sitting in the tent by the tunnel entrance while the others slept.

I was on the 3.00am shift one night, squatting by the tent tunnel in my sleeping bag, with one of the trusty bolt-action rifles in my lap. Given my lack of trained speed in handling such a weapon, I had a bullet 'up the spout' ready for action if necessary.

An hour is not usually very long to be on watch but, in that environment it was plenty long enough. My thoughts were alternating between a warm log fire and a big juicy steak, when I heard a snuffling outside the tent. Something or someone had clearly got telepathic reception of what I was cooking in my head.

I quietly put the rifle to my shoulder and took a deep breath. Whatever was outside was now slowly making its way into the tunnel. A moment later, I found myself face to face with a large wolf. It stopped momentarily when it saw me, about four feet away. I was taking no chances – I fired, and the loud crack of the shot in the quiet night seemed to bounce around the tent as all the men leapt up in temporary shock and confusion.

Cue an assortment of yelling, swearing, torches going on and general hoo-hah. As the pandemonium settled down, we inspected the body of the wolf, shot through the head, lying in the tunnel at my feet. We couldn't get out, so one of our neighbours dragged the body of the wolf out by its back legs.

When news of the incident got back to the base, it was decided to have a proper wolf hunt. This may seem strange nowadays, given the various projects to reintroduce wolves in many parts of the world. But back then, the wolf population was in plague proportions, killing off the local caribou which the locals relied on for their meat.

That was how I and the other British officers found ourselves lying on the open back ramp of a low-flying Chinook helicopter, shooting at wolves fifty feet below us.

Unfortunately, Lieutenant John Charteris took a break to relieve himself against the side wall, not realizing that his liquid output would promptly freeze on the ramp. As he picked his rifle back up, he slipped on the resulting ice. If the two people on either side of him had not been so alert, he would have slid off the back of a Chinook helicopter on his own pee. That would have been a unique death certificate.

*   *   *

At the end of our time in Canada, a chartered DC-7 from Caledonian Airlines arrived to fly us back to the UK. Presumably the RAF were terribly busy that week.

On their arrival, the flight crew stayed overnight and so we entertained the very attractive air hostesses during the evening, with some drinking and dancing. I stayed longer than most, but when the nice lady I was chatting to finally retired to her room, I thought I'd better do the same. I headed back to the room I shared with John Charteris and blundered in, only to find him entertaining one of the other hostesses … in *my* bed.

The next morning, terribly hung over, we boarded the DC-7 to fly back. We were all sitting in our seats, dozing off, when the captain came into the cabin.

'Has anyone seen our navigator? He's not turned up this morning.'

The navigator was eventually found asleep on the floor of an empty room in the Officers' Mess. We sobered him up as much as possible by applying coffee and threats, before taking him out to the aircraft. I think we flew home the long way around.

As a result of now being trained in temperatures as low as minus 45° centigrade, and fully qualified at enormous expense to the British taxpayer as an Arctic Warfare instructor, I was perfectly prepared to employ my new skills in my next exciting posting.

With typical Army wisdom, I was promptly posted to Aden in South Arabia, which could have daily highs of *plus* 45°.

Chapter 5

What Shell through Yonder Window Breaks?

The port city of Aden has been a strategic harbour for several millennia. It came under British rule in 1838 when a parcel of land, including a fishing village, was ceded to Britain by the ruling Sheikh of the area and the British East India Company landed Royal Marines in Aden to defend British shipping from pirates.

In December 1963, an insurgency against British administration known as the 'Aden Emergency' began with an attack by the communist National Liberation Front (NLF) on the British High Commissioner. Britain announced it would grant independence in four years' time, but the security situation deteriorated as the NLF and the FLOSY (Front for the Liberation of Occupied South Yemen) vied for control.

During the Aden Emergency, the Radfan Campaign was a series of British military actions in the mountainous Radfan region near the border with Yemen against local tribesmen connected with the NLF who were raiding the main road between Aden and the town of Dhala in Yemen. In January 1964 the Federal Regular Army (FRA)attempted to restore order, but in April British troops were also sent in.

On 30 November 1967 British troops were finally evacuated, leaving Aden under NLF control. The Royal Marines, in deference to the memory of the original troops deployed in 1839, were the last to leave.

I was posted to Aden in May 1964 with the 1st Battalion The Royal Scots. As one of only two officers who had completed the Forward Air Controller (FAC) training course, that became my operational role, much to my surprise and considerable apprehension.

On arrival at RAF Khormaksar in Aden I was met by Flight Lieutenant Bill Stoker. He was one hell of a character.

'Before you go up to the Radfan, youngster, I'm taking you up with me in a T7.'

The T7 was a two-seater trainer version of the single-seater Hawker Hunter fighter jet. As we performed various manoeuvres and dummy runs in the T7, I tried to keep my stomach from coming out of my ears while Bill gave me a lesson in local FAC tactics.

'Forget what you've been taught back in Chivenor. There are no landmarks up in the Radfan, it's all rocks and sand. Learn to use the colour of the terrain to control the strikes. Imagine what colours the pilot is seeing and describe the target position in those terms.'

After a few more stomach-churning runs, we thankfully started to head back to the airfield. We were just a few miles from base when Bill suddenly called out on the intercom.

'Smugglers! Arms smugglers!'

A line of over twenty heavily-laden camels was being led across the desert below. Bill radioed the grid reference back to RAF Khormaksar to send out a rapid reaction team by helicopter to capture the rebels. We circled at height for a minute or two but then, despite being in an unarmed T7, Bill decided to take matters into his own hands.

'Hang on, I'm going down to make them drop their loads.'

He then proceeded to make an extremely low-level pass. I could tell we were low because I was looking *up* in amazement at palm trees passing by the cockpit. The noise of the jet fighter caused mayhem in the line of camels as we screamed just over their heads, while the tribesmen took pot-shots at us with their rifles.

We climbed and circled again until we saw the arrival of the rapid reaction team, who recovered a large collection of British-made rifles, ammunition and landmines. I later learned that this ordnance had come from the British base at Tel El-Kabir in Egypt, which had been abandoned to the Egyptians at the end of the Suez Crisis. Due to the Egyptian backing of the NLF and FLOSY rebel groups, it was ironically now being supplied to the rebels to use against us.

*   *   *

Living under canvas is a regular occurrence in the Army and so is something you put up with, without question. However, my nine months in Aden put me off camping for life.

We had a total of four one-month operational tours 'up-country' in the mountains of the Radfan, interspersed with a month back in Aden. Unlike the King's Own Scottish Borderers, who were on a two-year accompanied posting and so lived in married quarters, we were just doing an emergency posting. That meant we had to live in tents not just while on operations up-country but also back in Aden, in a massive tented village known as 'Radfan camp' next to RAF Khormaksar. Officers shared four or six to a tent, which was pitched over a temporary concrete floor. We each had a camp bed, a wooden chest-of-drawers and a large suitcase. We had no formal clothing – just desert combat kit and a few items of civilian clothes. We often wore nothing but shorts.

The heat and humidity were oppressive. We preferred our monthly operational tours in the mountains because the temperature dropped at night. Down by the coast in Radfan camp, it usually exceeded 40° centigrade during the day, and barely cooled at all overnight.

But the humidity! On average we would sweat about 1.5 pints per hour, and the humidity meant it didn't evaporate. We had to drill holes in all the plastic seats to avoid sitting in salty puddles.

*   *   *

Sporadic rifle fire from the hostile local tribesmen, self-proclaimed as 'The Red Wolves of the Radfan', was an almost daily occurrence. It came from a distance, not terribly accurate and usually just before nightfall, due to the tribesmen quickly learning that our standard response of calling in a Hawker Hunter airstrike was much less effective in the failing evening light.

Despite the predictability and lack of accuracy of the tribesmen's fire, I had a rather lucky escape one afternoon. I was with my mortar section, having an early evening meal before taking up our defence positions. The ground was wet as we had just had a rare shower of rain, so to avoid the damp sand I was sitting on an A41 radio battery with my mess tin in my hands. Without warning, several rifles shots rang out, my legs went from under me and I fell to the ground, my first thought being that I had been hit.

I rolled on my side in the dust, looking for blood, but I could feel no pain. I yelled at the men to return fire and chase off the opportunist snipers. It was only when things had calmed down that I discovered that the radio battery between my legs had taken a direct hit from a bullet, utterly destroying it. That shower of rain saved my life, because had I been squatting in my usual position on the ground, the bullet would have killed me.

*   *   *

The frequency of evening attacks had been increasing, and so I was ordered to lay an ambush, to catch any baddies on their way to attack one of the British outposts. We chose a well-used pathway across a *wadi* and set up trip-flares on the opposite side, so that anyone triggering them would be silhouetted for us.

We had been waiting about three hours when a trip-flare suddenly went off – but we couldn't open fire as there was absolutely no one there to fire at. After a few more hours without further activity, we closed up shop and went back to the base, with the men moaning about faulty old flares.

Later that morning, we went back out to inspect the site and found the burnt-out flare and the two pegs and tripwire. We also spotted some large pugmarks in the mud. Being quite keen on such things, I cut one of the pugmarks out of the mud with a bayonet and put it in an old ration box to let it dry out.

I knew someone who worked at Aden University and so, on my return from that month's tour up-country, I went to show him what I had found. Humouring me, he offered to take my precious lump of mud to the Natural History department. The very next day, he came around to see me at the base. He was, to my surprise, rather excited.

'Charles, you will not believe what that pugmark is!'

'Er … OK, I won't. So, what is it?'

'It is the pugmark of an Arabian leopard. One hasn't been reported in this region for over sixty years. It was thought to be extinct!'

For my next tour up-country, the University supplied me with a special motion-detecting camera that would flash by night and hopefully take a photograph of the Arabian leopard. We set it up night after night after night but, sadly, our camera-shy leopard never returned.

*   *   *

Major Bob McCallum was keen to do some scouting beyond our front lines, to try to identify some long-range patrol routes. He managed to get hold of a Beaver aircraft piloted by a young Army Air Corps chap and then roped in my good friend Patrick Cardwell-Moore to go along as note-taker.

The trio had spent perhaps thirty minutes circling around the hills and valleys beyond our lines when the engine spluttered and cut out – no fuel! Directed by the Major, the young pilot headed for the nearest *wadi*, which was the only chance in such a rock-strewn environment to find a flat landing area. At least they knew that, with no fuel left, the chances of the plane bursting into flames in a crash-landing was greatly reduced.

Fortunately, the Beaver is known as a very hardy 'bush' aircraft, and the pilot managed a decent emergency landing in the dried-up riverbed. However, they were now in mortal danger, several miles beyond our lines, as any tribesmen in the area would undoubtedly have seen the aircraft coming down and would take pleasure in cutting them to pieces.

This is how Patrick recounted the story later that evening:

> We knew that ground troops would be on their way to recover us, or that we might even get a helicopter out. Once we had set off a smoke bomb to mark our location, the Major immediately asked us what ammunition we had. The pilot had an automatic pistol with ten rounds, and I had my SLR with fifteen. The Major just had his revolver with five rounds.
>
> Our strategy was simple. As I had the SLR, I would engage first, to try to hold the bad guys at a distance. Once I was out of ammo, if they came closer, the pilot would have a go with his pistol. Failing that, the Major was going to give them a couple of pops and then save the last three bullets for the three of us.

Thankfully, no such action was required, as one of our patrols got to them before any tribesmen appeared.

The Major wanted the Beaver to be recovered – there was nothing wrong with it, other than that it couldn't take off from the riverbed. We duly called in an RAF Belvedere helicopter, which was a huge twin-rotor monster. As it flew over our position, I directed the pilot down towards the recovery site. The Beaver was duly hooked up below the helicopter and slowly lifted out of the *wadi*.

However, as the huge helicopter climbed into the skies and accelerated away, the little Beaver aircraft's wings started to generate their own 'lift' from the passing airflow – and it started to rise of its own accord, closing the gap between it and the helicopter! Maybe the downdraft of the helicopter rotors would have counteracted the upthrust before they touched, but the RAF pilot was taking no chances of this unusual payload causing a disaster. He jettisoned it immediately, and the little aircraft spiralled down on to the rocks below, whereupon the second fuel tank exploded in a huge fireball.

Only then did we realize that the original engine failure must have been due to the young Beaver pilot forgetting to manually switch over the fuel tanks.

*   *   *

We were on our way back to Aden from our latest tour up-country in the Radfan region, when Archie Addison was approached by an Arab trying to sell him a baby baboon. Archie was a gung-ho fighter who had served in the British-formed paramilitary group known as the Trucial Oman Scouts. As a result, he was one of the very few of us who spoke excellent Arabic.

After much haggling and arguing in the local lingo, Archie proudly rejoined us with newly-named Baby Archie on his shoulder. Baby Archie was very tame and friendly, happily living with his adopted parent in his tent. He behaved like any young child – he played in the dirt, he didn't like to shower and occasionally he threw his food at you. He was also very loveable, and would hang around our tents looking for titbits or just wanting a hug.

One morning, Addison was called away on riot control in downtown Aden, so asked me to keep an eye on Baby Archie for the day. I wasn't going to waste my day off by hanging around the camp, so I put a makeshift collar and lead on Baby Archie, popped him into the back of a Land Rover and drove off to the beach with a few beers in a cool-box.

As Baby Archie and I lay on the sand sunning ourselves, I noticed how interested he was in the children playing on the beach. He had probably never seen small children like himself before. I could tell he was desperate to join in and, by the time I had finished my fourth beer, he had very eloquently convinced me to let him do just that.

I slipped his collar off, and Baby Archie cautiously wandered over to the children, who were delighted to see him. The parents around me were clearly a little nervous, but we all sat quite amazed as Baby Archie started to play with the children, building up mounds of sand to help with their sandcastles, grabbing the ball and throwing it back to them and even wandering into the sea for a cooling paddle and a game of splashing.

As the days rolled by, the more that Baby Archie interacted with us in camp, the more he became one of the family. Unfortunately, his friendliness got him into hot water early one morning.

We were all woken by yelling and shouting. Tumbling out of our beds, we emerged from our tents with pistols in hand, expecting the worst. Instead, we were met by the Colonel who had just come out of the toilet block with his trousers around his ankles and Baby Archie on his back, arms and legs wrapped around him, giving him the best of hugs.

Archie Addison was sent for. The Colonel in no uncertain terms made it clear that Baby Archie was not to be seen anywhere near the Officers' Lines again. Fortunately, the youngster had become a firm favourite with the troops and so was adopted by the Recce Platoon, who let him stay with them until the end of our posting.

*   *   *

I was with my mortar section at a village we called 'November 7' for the very imaginative reason that we had arrived there on that date. It started to rain. It typically only rained heavily a few days in the year, but when it did, it really rained. It came down so quickly and so heavily that the pits containing our mortars and ammunition rapidly filled up with water.

The village was deserted because the locals had been relocated as part of the process of trying to maintain peace in the area. The standing order was not to enter their empty houses, but I decided that, given the circumstances, it was a sensible thing to do.

I ordered a 'flash burn' of the nearest house. A 'flash burn' was a means of quickly clearing one of these small houses of mosquitoes, beetles and other bugs, by filling an empty can of cola with petrol and dribbling it along the floor around the inside walls. When a match was then put to the petrol, the brief 'whoomph' burst of flame was usually enough to clear the worst of the creepy-crawlies.

My corporal ordered one of the young soldiers to prepare the flash burn, but this youngster rather unfortunately mistook the instruction of 'a can of petrol' to mean a *jerry-can*. Unbeknown to me, he happily went all around this small house pouring 20 litres of petrol over the floor.

Not realizing his mistake, I walked up to the doorway intending to inspect the house before lighting the petrol. However, my dear corporal already had his box of matches at the ready and, as I approached the open entrance, he dropped a lit match through one of the side windows.

There was a violent explosion and I was blown backwards about thirty yards, landing in the mud in the middle of a cattle ring, which was a much softer landing than if I had just hit the hard dirt. I was also lucky that I was still dripping wet from the rain, which I'm sure saved me from worse injuries. Nevertheless, the flames had burnt all the exposed skin on my face and arms, and by all accounts I looked a done-for mess.

I was bundled into a Land Rover and driven back to the Company HQ about a mile away. We were met by the Company Commander, Major Jock Wilson-Smith.

'Give him a shot of morphia.'

'Yes, Sir, right away, Sir!.'

As the needle was being removed from my arm following the morphia shot, a voice called out to the Major.

'Sir – the doctor's on the radio. He says whatever you do, don't give the patient any morphia, it could kill him ...'

Unbeknown to the Major, morphia can affect your breathing, which can be lethal for burns patients if they have also suffered from smoke inhalation. I was unconscious at this point, having decided at some point in the proceedings that the game was surely up.

My colleagues also assumed the same and, as my body was being rather unceremoniously transferred into the cargo bin of an arriving Wessex helicopter, I was thoughtfully given the last rites by David Mehan, a devout Roman Catholic. During the helicopter flight back to Thumier, the Regimental Colonel was given the news of my demise by radio and promptly and very efficiently wrote a letter of condolence to my parents back in Scotland.

I regained a degree of consciousness as I was wheeled into the field hospital from the helicopter, although I could not move or speak. But I distinctly heard the doctor's first words as he took a look at me.

'My word, this chap Ritchie is still alive. His burns don't look too bad to me. Give him a shot of morphia.'

I wanted to yell out, but couldn't, and no one had thought to pin the obligatory label from the first injection on my collar, or mark the letter 'M' on my forehead – common ways to indicate morphia had been administered to a wounded soldier. Presumably they thought it was a rather redundant message to put on a corpse.

The second morphia shot promptly sent me into a coma.

Eventually, I came to, and the doctor was duly summoned.

'Ah, Lieutenant Ritchie, very pleased you're back with us. We'll get you out of here and flown back to Aden as soon as poss.'

In a state of morphine-induced euphoria, I didn't want to cause any more trouble and mumbled my best apology.

'Don't worry, doctor ... I'm sure I can make my own way there ...'

Fortunately, my drug-induced bravado was ignored. I was flown back to Aden and put in the only air-conditioned hospital ward in Steamer Point. There was only one other chap in the ward, who had just been brought in with much more severe burn injuries. His had been caused by, of all things, a bodged barbecue. That poor fellow did not survive the night.

Thankfully, I only needed a couple of weeks of recuperation before I was discharged – no bones broken, no skin-grafts required, and no lasting damage. An incredibly lucky young man.

Oh yes – and I managed to make a reassuring phone call to my parents before they received the Colonel's letter of condolence in the post.

* * *

For our third tour back up at the Radfan, we were based on a plateau known simply as 'Table-Top'.

We had a report that there were strange noises coming from one of the empty houses in the nearby village. I took a couple of men with me to investigate. We had to make sure that rebels were not looting or, more seriously, preparing an attack.

We approached the house cautiously and I called out a warning in what little Arabic I had. No one replied, but we could distinctly hear movement inside. I signalled to my two men to go around the back, while

I approached the front entrance. Once they were in position, I banged loudly on the flimsy wooden door, only to hear a loud crash as furniture was up-ended. 'Damn', I thought, 'they're getting ready to fire.'

I had my back to the wall, next to the door, thinking about my next move. The element of surprise was gone. Do I charge in and try to take them out, and risk getting shot? Do I come back with more men? I quickly fumbled in my webbing for a hand grenade, but only pulled out a small tin of biscuits.

Then there was a Glaswegian shout from the back of the house.

'Aww, hey, Sir! Ah kin see through the windae – it's a coo, so it is!'

We had a variety of nicknames and euphemisms for rebel tribesmen, but I was pretty sure 'coo' wasn't one of them. Gathering up my dignity, I marched into the house and promptly arrested the cow, which had illegally broken into the house and was eating the furniture.

Jessie the cow quickly became an established member of our camp up-country. She was very well looked after until the villagers returned and she was reunited with her owner.

*   *   *

A week later, one of our night patrols reported seeing a light flashing inside one of the empty mud and stone houses in a village about two miles from our camp. Ruling out the option that one of Jessie's friends had come looking for her by torchlight, our assumption was that rebel tribesmen were coming into the village at night in preparation for their regular sniper attacks on us.

I was ordered to go out in the late afternoon with some of my platoon to tackle the baddies when they arrived. I should have been more suspicious when we got to the house and found the door bolted from the inside. I used a bayonet to simply slide back the bolt, entered and searched the house – nobody there.

We set ourselves up at the firing slits which served as windows in these buildings, re-bolted the door and waited. Absolutely nothing happened.

At daybreak, we put the house back as we had found it, packed up and returned to camp, reporting that it had been a complete waste of time.

A few weeks later, we were back again on our final tour up-country. By this stage, a form of peace had broken out and we were on speaking terms with the local tribe, who took great pleasure in updating us, via our interpreter, on our previous visit.

'You went into a house in this village last month to set up an ambush.'

'Yes, we did, but nothing happened.'

'It was bolted from the inside.'

'Yes, but we searched the house, there was no one there.'

'You did not search properly. Below the ground floor is the grain store. That is where eight men hid while you were above them.'

We had unwittingly spent the night directly above a group of armed tribesmen. They would certainly have tried to kill us if they had had the chance.

*   *   *

Our Arab guide from the FRA came to me one day with a complaint. He was unhappy with our use of batmen for, as he put it, the purposes of manservants.

'Lieutenant Ritchie – a soldier should not be a manservant. A soldier should not have to make tea and wake up his colleagues. A soldier should not have to clean another man's boots.'

There were very few batting duties while on an operational tour, but nevertheless this was a brave attack on centuries of British Army tradition. There must be a reason, I thought, behind this bare-faced cheek.

'What do you suggest?'

'My brother will do it. Seven days a week. For one dinar per week.'

'Deal.'

The next day, our Arab guide arrived with a very young boy in tow.

'Lieutenant Ritchie, here is my brother Raga.'

'Good grief – how old is he?'

'Sir, he is already eight years old.'

'I cannot possibly employ an eight-year-old boy!'

Arab men have a wonderful way of looking mortally offended at the slightest of slights. His look of indignation and disgust at my unethical backtracking was award-winning.

He drew himself up to his full five feet and two inches.

'Lieutenant Ritchie – as a British officer, you gave your word that you would employ my brother as a manservant for one dinar per week.'

'Yes ... but ... you didn't tell me how old he was!'

'Lieutenant Ritchie – you did not ask me how old my brother was.'

Raga got the job and, in addition to his one dinar per week – equivalent to £1 sterling – he went home each evening with as much tinned food as he could carry.

*   *   *

The very next day a local woman asked to see me, accompanied by the translator.

'Sir – I understand that you have a combat soldier to clean the pots and dishes in your cookhouse.'

I could see what was coming.

'And I suppose you believe a soldier should not be used to clean pots?'

'Indeed, Sir, a soldier should not clean pots.'

'What do you suggest?'

'I have a son who will do that for you, seven days per week, for one and a half dinar per week.'

Once bitten, twice shy.

'How old is your son?'

'Sir, he is fourteen years old.'

I took the teenager to see Cook Sergeant Walls, lovingly known as Porky Walls. He was a tough Scot who was none too impressed with our potential recruit.

'Sir, I hope ye dinna mind ma sayin' it, but yon laddie's a manky tattie-bogle – mair glaur on him than a midden.'

'All right, Sergeant – get him in the shower, while I find him some clean clothes.'

I was gathering together an army shirt, a pair of shorts, gym shoes and socks, when I heard almighty screaming. It was coming from the spa and shower block, which comprised a tarpaulin-walled square with a bucket rigged up overhead.

I set off running, accompanied by the translator. I knew Porky Walls hadn't been back to Glasgow to see his wife for over eight months, but what on earth was he doing to that nice young boy?

The yelling was indeed coming from our new pot-washer as he stood inside the shower, with lukewarm water pouring down on him and a subsequent stream of filthy water exiting from the drain below.

'Sergeant Walls, what on earth is his problem?'

'Ah dunno, Sir.'

The translator, meanwhile, was grinning.

'Ah, you British, you are so cruel!'

'What do you mean, cruel? We're trying to help the lad!'

'This boy is only fourteen years old. He is terrified. He has never had a shower in his life.'

*　*　*

A breathless Jock ran up to me one morning.

'Sir, we've got a problem. The villagers' corn is being stolen!'

The village crop of corn was a vital part of their meagre existence, and so we had to protect the crops just as much as the villagers themselves. I hurried over to take a look for myself.

'Hang on – those aren't people!'

'No, Sir. They're baboons.'

A troop of baboons was indeed busily helping themselves to the corn.

I ordered our brave soldiers to scare the thieves away, so they dutifully proceeded to hurl rocks, sticks and their best Scottish insults. The baboons stopped, turned to face us – and started throwing the rocks back with, it has to be said, a great deal more accuracy.

It was the only time in my career that I ordered a retreat. And it was from an enemy troop of baboons.

*　*　*

Jebel Widina was a large mountainous area in the Radfan region. A troublesome tribe lived at the top of the mountain, which was a flat plateau about a mile long and half a mile wide. Travelling caravans would wend their way up the side of the mountain to visit the tribe and trade in livestock, food – and weaponry. The tribesmen would then use their mountaintop as the ideal location from which to carry out raids, as well as simply taking pot-shots down across the valley.

The Army decided that this troublesome tribe had to be removed to a different location. A ground-based attack up the mountain was out of the question, so it was decided by some gung-ho madman back at base that we would mount a dawn raid using fighter jets and five Scout helicopters, each carrying three machine-gunners and a heap of ammunition. The plan was to deploy such a show of force that the tribesmen would not dare attack but would instead scarper off the mountain. The glaring flaw in the plan, as I saw it, was that it needed an FAC to go along to direct the aircraft.

As we set off early one morning, the near-death experience on Sidbury Hill was fresh in my memory. Many years later, when I saw the helicopter scene from the film *Apocalypse Now*, I couldn't help but think back to that dawn helicopter ride to Jebel Widina, although I suspect the music in my head that morning was not *Ride of the Valkyries* but maybe something like the Beatles No. 1 song at the time – *Help!*

The helicopters went in first and landed in darkness at one end of the plateau. We deployed the machine-gunners, and the helicopters promptly headed back to camp for breakfast. In the pre-dawn silence, it was a strange feeling – the fifteen soldiers, the Major and me, about to face upwards of 400 armed tribesmen.

At dawn, the first tribesmen showed up at our end of the mountaintop. We let loose with machine gun fire over their heads and I called in the fighter airstrikes to complete the show of force. To our relief, the plan worked. Over the next few hours, we saw the tribesmen gather up and head off down the mountain. We secured the whole area, and the next day, the rest of our force of over 100 men was brought in on two of the huge double-rotor Belvedere helicopters.

The accommodation wasn't up to much. We camped inside *sangars*, which were simply temporary fortifications of boulders, as it was hopeless to try to dig trenches in the rocky ground. We also had to maintain a constant watch with round-the-clock sentries.

*   *   *

On the second night on Jebel Widina there was a sudden burst of shouting and yelling from one of the sentry-posts. I ran out from my *sangar* to find out what was going on. One of the sentries pointed at a cave about 50 yards away, claiming he had seen a ghost.

'What are you talking about, man?'

'Sir, ah swear oan ma life – a ghost just came oot o' that cave! A grey auld man wi' a long white beard.'

Once things settled down again, I decided to join the next watch, armed with a powerful torch. While the sentries watched the approaches to the mountain top, I kept my eyes on the cave.

After a while, to my amazement, a ghostly figure appeared at the cave entrance. It was a stooped old grey man with a beard, just as the sentry had described. My heart was suddenly pounding, but I shone my torch directly at the ghost, which stopped and stared back.

It was a baboon – a very old baboon that had either been left behind by its troop or had made its own choice to live alone.

For the rest of our stint on Jebel Widina, the baboon became our unofficial mascot and was well fed and watered, although it still only ever came out of its cave at night.

*   *   *

Every Sunday, the Roman Catholic chaplain would arrive at our base camp in the mountains by armoured car, accompanied by our Church of Scotland minister.

The RC chaplain was a really gregarious, outgoing young chap. On his first visit, I gathered our four Catholic soldiers for him, and he held a small service for them at one end of our camp, from where I could hear laughter and frivolity. Meanwhile, the rest of the mostly Protestant company gathered around our minister at the other end and were subjected to a fire-and-brimstone sermon that threatened us all with everlasting hell and damnation for our many sins.

The next Sunday, when I gathered the men for the arrival of the clergy, the Catholic ranks had swelled to eight; the following Sunday to over a dozen; and the week after, it was approaching twenty. Clearly, the RC chaplain was a charming and engaging talker, but this degree of religious conversion would have been remarkable even for Mary Tudor. Something else was going on.

As the chaplain was saying goodbye and warmly shaking the hands of his ever-growing flock at the end of his service, I collared one of them who I knew was an avid Glasgow Rangers fan and therefore not the most likely of converts.

'So, MacLeod – how was the chaplain's service today?'

'Aye, Sir, it wuz grand, so it wuz.'

The whiff on his breath was unmistakable, but alcohol was expressly forbidden while on operational duty 'up-country'. After a brief bollocking and a couple of threats, Private MacLeod spilled the beans. It turned out that the young chaplain always carried some alcoholic refreshment with him as he did his tour around the various outposts and was in the habit of being quite liberal in sharing it with his congregation.

* * *

In a rare demonstration of combined forces, we were attacked one early evening by a total of around 100 tribesmen. This was by some distance the most significant military action in Aden that my Company was involved in.

It was approaching 5.00pm. We were just about to take up our defensive positions to protect ourselves from the usual evening pot-shots, when we heard the 'ping ... ping' of two ranging shots. Then all hell broke loose as this large mass of tribesmen all opened fire at once. The soldier next to me got a bullet across the back of his head, and another man was shot through the thigh. I pulled them both into cover in our *sangar* while we returned fire with everything we had.

We were pinned down and in a spot of bother. However, we had an Observation Point (OP) out on one of the neighbouring hills. During a pause in the gunfire, our guy at the OP about a mile away radioed in.

'Hello, Zero, you won't believe this, but they are starting to gather in X-Ray 22.'

X-Ray 22 was a position on the map that we happened to be already ranged in to with our mortars and artillery, from our most recent training exercise. I simply shouted out the order.

'Mortars ... Artillery ... X-Ray 22!'

'Ready, Sir!'

'Ready, Sir'

'Fire!'

We fired rapid mortars and rapid artillery, and the rounds landed in the middle of where the tribesmen were assembling.

After a brief barrage, I ordered the cease fire to check what was happening. We watched with interest as three tribesmen came in with a white flag. I brought our interpreter forward.

'What do they want?'

'They want to take their dead and wounded away.'

'Only if they will sign a piece of paper to certify they will never come back and shoot at us again.'

After a period, the interpreter came back.

'I have spoken to the tribal chief. They cannot do that.'

'In that case, those bodies will have to lie there and be eaten by wild pig during the night.'

More debate followed, and a ceasefire was called. An agreement was subsequently drawn up and signed, and that was the last time we were shot at – and the last time they lost any of their tribesmen.

*   *   *

We were on our fourth and final one-month stint up-country, based again at Table-Top. We were hoping for a quiet time, given that the two local tribes, the Hujaili and the Ibdali, had both made peace.

However, a report came in of activity at one of the empty Ibdali villages, to which the local population had not yet returned, below Table-Top . As we approached, we could see a group of what turned out to be Hujaili opportunists entering each village house and removing the sacks of winter grain from the cellars.

We clearly had to stop this. Being a reasonable sort of chap, I ordered a quick burst of machine gun fire over their heads to get their attention. They meekly walked over to our position with their hands up. I singled out the ringleader and then radioed the Political Officer for instructions.

Political Officers at the time were members of the Colonial Office who, due to the sensitive political situation, had to authorize all British Army actions during the Radfan campaign. They were all suspected of being officers of MI6, but this was never publicly admitted.

'Hello, Sir, it's Lieutenant Ritchie here.'

'Yes, yes, what is it, boy?'

'Sir, we've caught a whole lot of Hujaili stealing the winter grain stores from the Ibdali tribe.'

'Is there a ringleader?'

'Yes, sir, there is a very bolshie ringleader.'

'Right – take your interpreter with you, go to his village, get everybody gathered in front of the head man of the village, and give everyone a bollocking. Then blow the ringleader's house up.'

There was a pause. I was taken aback by this suggestion.

'Sir – I'll do no such thing.'

'You will do what you are f***ing well told, boy!'

Another pause. I needed to find a way to object.

'I'm sorry sir, but I don't take orders from civilians.'

'How dare you! Your Commanding Officer will hear about this IMMEDIATELY!'

The Political Officer was based at the Battalion HQ, right next to our CO's office. I heard some shouting at the other end of the phone and then the unmistakable voice of Lieutenant Colonel Charles Taylor came down the line.

'Ritchie, did you hear what the PO said?'

'Yes, Sir.'

'Then do as he says.'

Despite my tender years, I felt it necessary to make a stand.

'With the greatest respect, Sir – I did not join the British Army to blow up a family's house.'

'Oh for heaven's sake, do what he says, Ritchie! That's a direct order!'

'Very well, Sir – but I do so under protest. I thought this was what the Nazis did in France.'

Stunned silence for a moment.

'Charles Ritchie – if you ever thought you were going to have a successful career in the Army, you can forget it.'

Feeling pretty rotten about all this, I traipsed off to the village with about twenty of my heavily-armed Jocks. We gathered all the men and boys, while the wives and daughters stayed indoors, peering out of the firing slits in their houses.

As ordered, I used our interpreter to give them a bollocking about stealing the grain from the next door tribe. I then let the ringleader of the grain-stealing party and his family take all their possessions out of his house, before we placed 2lb explosive charges at each interior corner of the building and blew it up.

When the dust had literally settled, I had an idea. The Royal Engineers had recently built a bridge next to our position and had left a whole lot of unused teak timbers behind. Through the interpreter, I told the ringleader that he could take the leftover teak, with my permission, in order to help him rebuild a house for his family.

He took me at my word. All the wood quickly vanished, and within a week he had the best house in the village. Through our interpreter, the man's wife and daughters thanked me profusely as they moved into their new house, and I had several requests from other villagers to please come and blow up their house too.

* * *

As part of the ongoing relationship-building with the Federal Regular Army, we had a visit to our base at Table-Top from some of their senior officers. One chap, a Major, was particularly interested in what we had been doing in the Radfan and seemed very knowledgeable about the local geography and the challenging terrain.

I was commanding a battery of 105mm artillery at the time, as well as my own mortar platoon, so was given the job of putting on a display of our military might for the assembled officers. After warming them up with a display of our mortar-bomb accuracy, I proceeded to deafen them with a quick barrage from our 105mm pack howitzers on to a remote hillside.

Then came the highlight. We had got hold of one of the new lightweight WOMBAT anti-tank weapons that fired a hefty 120mm shell up to 1,000 yards with great accuracy. We didn't have to face many tanks in the Radfan, but this little monster could make short work of any stone fortification. To demonstrate its power and accuracy, I asked our lads to fire a shell through the window of a deserted building about 600 yards away. They did as they were asked, and the shell flew straight and true, disappeared through the window and produced an explosion that turned the building to rubble.

I triumphantly turned to our guests, expecting applause or at least some appreciative nods and smiles, but only got a stunned silence. Eventually, their Major spoke up.

'Lieutenant Ritchie, that was not very clever.'

'Really? Why not, sir?'

'Because that building was mine.'

The Major was indeed a local, and I had helpfully just blown up one of his properties. We had not come across any members of the FRA from the Radfan area before. The Army had to reimburse the Major, and our shiny new WOMBAT was taken off our hands, never to be returned.

*   *   *

The recce platoon was the best platoon in the Battalion and so was typically given the toughest or most dangerous tasks. However, due to their normal Platoon Commander getting his girlfriend pregnant and being posted home, I was temporarily placed in charge.

Quickly realizing their mistake, the most perilous thing my line of command ordered me to do with the recce platoon was to take them on a cruise up the Persian Gulf on HMS *Sir Lancelot*, which was a spanking new class of landing ship that had only just been commissioned. The idea was to give some army units early experience of the new ship.

The recce platoon and I took full advantage, bronzing ourselves every day on the ship's impressive sundeck, which the Royal Navy insisted on calling a helicopter pad.

Towards the end of our cruise, it was announced that we would be spending the night off the ship, at a training camp on a nearby beach. It was a decent camp with proper tents and beds, rather than the *sangars* we were used to up in the Radfan, but it was unbelievably hot, even during the night. We decided the best course of action was to carry our beds into the sea to cool off, which was lovely.

In the course of the night, as the tide receded, the beach was crawling with enormous crabs. They were tricky to catch, and had massive claws, so I ended up using my pistol. In those days, Lieutenants were not issued with army revolvers and we had to buy our own. I had procured my First World War German Luger 9mm automatic in Dicksons of Frederick Street in Edinburgh, for the princely sum of £20. It was fun to put it to some use.

*   *   *

The delicious crabs were thankfully the only casualties of my Luger during my time in Aden. In fact, the only other time I had cause to fire my trusty pistol was in an off-the-cuff rescue incident.

I was downtown in Aden, at Steamer Point, to get my camera repaired. The back streets of Aden were known to be quite dangerous, so I kept my eyes peeled. Heading back to base, I passed a small alleyway where I saw a British sailor being dragged along semi-conscious by a couple of local men. I yelled out something in Arabic, drew my Luger, and fired a shot over their heads, at which point they promptly ran off.

As I was trying to help the sailor to his feet, a crowd quickly gathered. I was relieved that my jolly jack-tar was uninjured, but rather dismayed to find that he was very jolly indeed. Drunk as a skunk would be more accurate.

Eventually, I managed to half-carry, half-drag him to the local police station for safety, where they simply stuck him in a cell until he sobered up. The next day, I was treated to a very nice little party on board his ship, as a thank-you for the rescue mission.

*   *   *

I was enjoying myself one day on a very busy Tarshyne beach in Aden when a Land Rover roared up and a soldier jumped out, yelling for me among the crowds.

'Sir, I have to take you back to camp immediately. They urgently need an FAC at Harib.'

We roared back to camp, I packed my bag, grabbed my rifle and an A43R ground-to-air radio, and was then driven over to RAF Khormaksar. Within minutes I was climbing into a waiting Twin Pioneer aircraft, known as a 'Twin Pin' – a Short Take-Off and Landing (STOL) aircraft that could operate on an airstrip no larger than 900ft by 100ft. Ideal for use in the terrain around Aden.

The flight to Harib was quick and uneventful, but as we made our approach to the landing strip, things quickly changed. The pilot turned and yelled to me.

'Get ready to jump out when we land, we're not stopping – we'll throw your kit out.'

'Why can't you stop?'

'They're shooting at the airstrip!'

I grabbed my rifle and radio in readiness, the plane bounced down on to the landing strip and when the pilot yelled to me, I leapt out of the moving plane as it taxied along. As bullets whizzed around me, I heard shouting from the far side of the runway.

'Lieutenant Ritchie! Over here! Over here!'

I ran for my life across to the field base and got safely inside.

'I didn't expect this sort of welcome!'

'Yes, it's getting a bit serious around here. But don't worry, we'll recover your pack and webbing after dark. In the meantime, come with us to get briefed.'

During a rather unappetizing lunch of goat and rice, it was explained to me that the Egyptian Army was probably going to invade – a serious escalation. A fort near the village of Harib was being used as a centre for distribution of arms across the frontier, as well as the HQ for incursions by Egyptian-armed nationalist tribesmen. Most recently, Egyptian-piloted jets had strafed a Federal fort at Jabal Dulaiq. Plans for retaliation were still being drawn up and so, after an evening meal of more goat and rice, I retired for the night.

I was awake bright and early the next morning. Breakfast was a huge disappointment, however – goat and rice. I raised my concerns politely with the mess sergeant.

More disappointment was to come. Despite having rushed in at a moment's notice, I was left kicking my heels for the whole day. The sensitive political nature of this crisis was causing a hiatus while the politicians debated what any British retaliation would do to the United Nations' security system. Meanwhile, I was becoming increasingly concerned about what all the goat meat was doing to my digestive system.

What I didn't know was that there were 25,000 Egyptian troops, plus money and supplies, lined up for a potential invasion. The mess sergeant didn't know this either, because the next morning he proudly presented me with a box of cornflakes, which he had obtained from the village across the border by walking across our defensive minefield in civilian clothes. What a star.

It was finally decided, at the highest levels in London, that a retaliatory airstrike as a show of force was necessary, despite the political risks. Hence yours truly found himself as the FAC preparing to direct an RAF strike on a foreign territory – a very rare action, and one that was about to cause a political storm back in the UK and in the United Nations.

We followed standard practice and dropped leaflets to warn the local villagers 24 hours before the planned strike, although Fort Harib itself was a mile and a half from the village. On the morning of the operation itself, eight Hunter fighters flew up from Aden and we did a final leaflet run on the fort itself to tell all the occupants to leave immediately. We then executed the attack, which involved rockets and machine-gun fire. The fort did have anti-aircraft guns, but they only put up a token resistance, their shells either exploding at completely the wrong height or not at all.

At the end of the day, we were ordered to collect some of the unexploded anti-aircraft shells. I was told by the local Political Officer to take a couple of these back to Aden in a rucksack, as the technical boys would be very interested in having a look at them.

My return journey was via a bumpy two-hour drive across the desert with the Political Officer to his base, from where I returned to Aden on a scheduled DC-3 flight. On arrival, I was met at the airport and driven to HQ for a debrief, at which I emptied my rucksack and proudly showed the shells I had brought back.

After a bit of head-scratching, a technical expert was called for. As soon as he came in and saw my hand-delivered ordnance he went bright red and spluttered some orders.

'Get me two fire-buckets right away – the rest of you, don't move a muscle!'

The fire-buckets were duly brought in and the shells were carefully placed in them. I then got one of the worst rollockings of my life:

'Ritchie, you are a complete and utter idiot. These shells have altitude detonators – you're damn lucky the DC-3 flies at a low altitude on short flights. If it had flown higher these could have exploded and killed you and everyone on that flight.'

Oops.

Chapter 6

Once More unto the Beach

Back in the day, most Australian State Governors were retired senior British Army officers. Each Governor was entitled to have two British Army Aides de Camp (ADCs), each of whom would do a two-year tour of duty with their Governor.

My two-year stint as an ADC was in the service of Major General Sir Rohan Delacombe. Sir Rohan had served in The Royal Scots with my father and so, although there were several young officers in the running for this rather desirable posting, I did perhaps have an edge on the competition. I'm sure it was also nothing to do with the Governor's wife being my godmother.

The two ADCs to a State Governor typically alternated between two days 'in attendance', and two days 'off'. When 'in attendance', you went to every single event that the Governor attended. Many of the two days supposedly 'off' were actually spent in performing reconnaissance and writing up the programme for future events.

I lived on the top floor of Government House in Melbourne, with a shared bathroom and a large bedroom, but no air conditioning. I used to leave the window open, and a possum would occasionally climb up the tree outside my window, hop into my room, sit on my mantelpiece and chatter to me.

* * *

One of the duties of the ADC at VIP dinners is to propose the toast to the reigning British monarch. At my first VIP dinner, I was incredibly nervous. I'd faced a few tricky situations already in my young life, but for some reason the pomp and ceremony of the situation got to me, and instead of referring to the Governor as 'Your Excellency', I accidentally promoted him to 'Your Majesty'.

At the second dinner a few days later, I decided that some Dutch courage was in order and so had a glass or three to calm my nerves. As a result, I got a little closer to the mark and managed to call him 'Your Ecstasy'.

The third time, I finally got the Governor's title spot-on. The immediate sense of relief gave me a hot flush and I barrelled on to propose the toast 'to Her Majesty, Queen Victoria'. An easy mistake to make, I felt, given that the host was the Governor of the State of Victoria. How I wasn't sacked or sent to the Tower, I'll never know.

*   *   *

One of the ADCs' time-consuming responsibilities was to write speeches for the Governor, which he then simply read out verbatim at each event. We would request notes in advance from the event's host, to provide local information and facts, but then we had to laboriously type these up in a fully readable form for the Governor.

I thought it would be much easier if we could get the Governor to speak directly from the notes we received, to cut out the work of yours truly as the middleman. However, although he had many talents, speaking from notes rather than reading verbatim was not something that my boss was very practised or proficient at doing. My fellow ADC, who had been in his post a year longer than me, thought there was no chance of the Governor buying this idea.

'A bottle of scotch says you'll fail.'

'You're on.'

I put my plan into action the very next week. We were attending the World Photographic Exhibition at Warrnambool. It was a more relaxed affair than most events the Governor attended, and so I had convinced him that, just this once, he should try talking from my short-style notes, to make his speech more natural and 'off-the-cuff'.

As part of my plan, during the pre-speech drinks I chatted to as many attendees as I dared, encouraging them to approach the Governor afterwards and congratulate him on his speech, as 'it is something that people rarely do, and it would be greatly appreciated'.

The Governor duly went ahead and had a go at giving his speech using just the notes. In all honesty it was not terribly good but, lo and behold, afterwards he was surrounded by people telling him how wonderful it was.

In the car on the way back to Government House, still flushed with his success, the Governor turned to me.

'Charles – from now on, I don't want speeches written in full. I will simply talk off notes that you give me, because clearly it is a much better way of doing things.'

* * *

The Governor came in one day and stared at the wall of our office, on which was hung a huge map of Victoria – the state, that is, not the monarch.

'When did a Governor last visit the Shire of Wycheproof?'

'I have no idea, your Excellency, but I will go and find out.'

I went to the office where all the records were kept, to see a very efficient lady called Fran Matthews.

'Oh yes Charles, let me see … ah, a Governor has not been there since 1947.'

I went back and told the Governor the news.

'Hmm, not good. Arrange a visit immediately!'

I rang up the Shire Secretary of the Shire of Wycheproof.

'Hello, Sir – Captain Charles Ritchie here. I am the ADC to his Excellency the Governor.'

'Ah, g'day – and how's old Sir Dallas?'

'Er … Sir Dallas Brookes retired some time ago. The new Governor, Major General Sir Rohan Delacombe, would like to visit the Shire of Wycheproof.'

'No worries!'

'Excellent. When would be convenient?'

'Strewth, mate – any time. Nothing ever happens up 'ere y'know.'

A few days later, to recce and plan the visit, I drove all the way up to the Shire of Wycheproof, about 200 miles north-west of Melbourne. The land was flat, practically desert and, appropriately, quite deserted.

Thankfully, I found two locations which could give us something for the Governor to visit, in the form of a stud farm for Merino sheep and a wheat research station. I also met the Shire President, the equivalent of a Lord Lieutenant in the UK, who was a very, very large man. He had a crucial question for me.

'Captain Ritchie – for the Governor's visit, my wife has asked me to ask you how to do a curtsy. Can you demonstrate?'

I duly demonstrated how a lady would make a curtsy to his Excellency the Governor.

'Thanks, Captain – now, I 'ave to admit, I've nevva made a speech in me life. Any advice on what to say for when the Guv'nor comes?'

As it happened, I had a copy in my briefcase of a speech that had been given a couple of weeks ago at a visit somewhere in the south of the state, so I gave him that to study as a sample. He was very grateful.

One month later, the Governor and I took the train from Melbourne up to Wycheproof. As we stepped off the train, we were met by the Shire President and a line-up of local dignitaries. I duly began to make the formal introductions.

'Your Excellency, may I have the honour to present Councillor Widgeree, the Shire President of the Shire of Wycheproof?'

The Shire President blushed profusely and, despite his enormous size, proceeded to perform a faultless curtsy.

Horrified, I quickly hurried down the line in front of the Governor, whispering as loudly as I dared.

'Only ladies curtsy. Gentlemen just nod your head!'

Further embarrassment averted, we then headed to a stage at the front of the Town Hall, where it seemed the whole population of Wycheproof had gathered to witness this great visit. Once everyone was settled, the Shire President stood up and began his speech.

'Your Excellency, on behalf of the people of the Shire, I welcome you to the green rolling hills of the largest butter-producing Shire in the country.'

The entire crowd burst out laughing at this strange description of their flat-as-a-pancake, near-desert homeland.

Undeterred, the President ploughed on with an even more bizarre proclamation.

'I would like to thank the Governor for unveiling a plaque to commemorate the opening of the town's wonderful new Olympic swimming pool.'

This caused even greater mirth in the audience, whose local billabong was presumably as dry as my mouth had just become.

'Charles – what the hell is going on? First this man curtsies to me – and now he's going on about opening some damn swimming pool?

I had to explain that the poor Shire President had obviously taken the sample speech I had given him from a different Shire visit, learned it by heart, and was now regurgitating it verbatim. We sat with grim smiles while the poor fellow gamely finished his speech and the locals laughed until they wept.

The Governor was a patient man, but this tested him to the limit.

'Charles – if anything remotely like this ever happens again, you're on the next plane home.'

Thankfully, it didn't. How could it?

*   *   *

Annabelle Wood was a lovely girl I knew during my time in Melbourne. Annabelle's father was a very influential businessman who, among other things, was responsible for running Melbourne Racecourse. He had organized two tickets for Annabelle to see the Rolling Stones during their tour of Australia in 1966 and very kindly gave them to me on two conditions: I had to tell Annabelle that I had acquired them myself rather than from him, and I had to bring his daughter back for a family dinner afterwards.

I escorted a delighted Annabelle to the concert, where we had a great time. Afterwards, we collected the car and drove back to her parents' house. We parked outside next to some large, flashy cars I didn't recognize but, thinking nothing of it, we walked into the drawing room to find the Rolling Stones, in person, all standing around having a pre-dinner chat with selected guests. Clearly, Annabelle's father was a man of some influence.

At dinner I was sat next to Bill Wyman – a charming fellow, but not the most outgoing of the band members. Nevertheless, he was a very engaging and friendly chap.

*   *   *

Many years later, while I was based back in Tidworth, I was sent to London to attend a Memorial Service in Westminster Abbey. Along with seven fellow officers, all in Number 1 Dress uniforms, I travelled by train from Tidworth to London and back.

On the way back we all needed a drink, so I headed off to see if there was a bar. It was the rule in those days that you had to travel first class when wearing ceremonial uniform, and on the Waterloo to Andover service there was a very nice first class saloon carriage. There, on his own, was none other than Bill Wyman. I recognized him immediately from the dinner I had attended in Melbourne years earlier.

'Mr Wyman, you won't remember me – Captain Charles Ritchie of The Royal Scots. We met in Melbourne in 1966; we dined together at the Woods' house after your concert.'

To my delight, he did remember – or at least, he graciously pretended to. He asked if I would join him but I declined, explaining the reason for the dress uniform and that I had seven colleagues with me. On hearing the story, he immediately instructed the barman.

'There are eight young officers in ceremonial uniform on this train. Make sure they have unlimited champagne from here to Andover.'

Delighted, I brought the others to the bar and, needless to say, we all had a terrific time all the way back to Tidworth, drinking copious amounts of champagne while the charming Bill Wyman regaled us with eye-watering stories of his rock 'n' roll life.

* * *

We had the Australian Governor General of Papua New Guinea come down to Melbourne and stay for the Melbourne Cup – Australia's equivalent of Royal Ascot week. I got to know him and his wife very well and, at the end of his visit, he invited me to visit the capital, Port Moresby.

'Come for a week – I will fix it all up for you.'

I flew direct from Darwin to Port Moresby, where I was received by the local ADC and spent one night in the capital's downtown region.

I was introduced to a charming recruiting officer for the Royal Pacific Islands Regiment who flew himself around in a light plane. He was due to make a recruitment tour around all parts of Papua New Guinea, and the poor fellow had been ordered by the Governor to take this silly young British Army Captain with him on his trip.

But first, there was the small matter of a golf match against the Royal Australian Air Force.

'Do you play golf, Charles?'

'Yes. Badly.'

'Never mind, you're now in the Australian Army team.'

We arrived next morning at Royal Port Moresby Golf Club, which in those days was situated on a rather swampy low-lying piece of land. I believe it has since moved to a site slightly more suitable for golf.

'Charles, here's a set of clubs, and your caddie – and your ball-boy.'

'I beg your pardon – a ball-boy? For golf? What does the ball-boy do?'

'Well, what you do is tell him how far you are likely to hit the ball. He then goes down the fairway that distance and stands waiting for your ball to arrive, to stop it being pinched by the local birds, or by youngsters who will sell it back to you at the clubhouse at the end of your round.'

This was going to be challenging – both for me and my ball-boy.

I managed to get my first shot a decent distance down the first hole, but not very straight – into the rough on the right. My ball-boy trotted off to the edge of the fairway next to where my ball had disappeared into the long grass, but he stopped there and put a marker down.

'Bad luck Charles – two shot penalty there, you can't go into the rough.'

'Why ever not?'

'Crawling with poisonous snakes, I'm afraid.'

Not surprisingly, I went through a fair number of golf balls that morning – although I'm pretty sure my ball-boy nipped back later to collect them, poisonous snakes or not!

*   *   *

The next day, we set off on our flying tour. Due to its inhospitable terrain, the country has a very diverse population. Tribes only a few miles apart have completely unique customs and beliefs.

At one village 'court' in a very remote part of the country, I discovered one remarkable local practice: no one was allowed to have sex for six years after having a child, with the result that all the children were born in groups six years apart. I never learned how or why this local law had come about!

Most memorably, we visited a place called Nomad River, where I stayed with a gentleman called the Patrol Officer. I took a photograph of the police officers with some prisoners.

'What are these chaps in for?'

There was a rather uncomfortable pause.

'Well … we don't normally tell visitors but … as you are a military man, you will understand. We are working to try to stop murder and cannibalism. At the moment, the going rate for those we catch is one month for eating human flesh, and one year for murder.'

I made some comment about the perspective on the degree of the punishment and then asked my host an even more insensitive question.

'Have you ever eaten human flesh?'

'Ah, well … it's like this. When you visit a new tribe, the greatest honour they can give you is to have a tribal fight with the tribe next door. These fights last three days. Day one, they paint up and stick feathers in their hair, and chant and sing; day two, they fight; and day three, they all sit down to a feast and discuss who owes what to whom, depending on how the fight went. And yes, as part of one of these visits, I have once eaten human flesh.'

'And … ?'

'Tastes like roast pork cooked in golden syrup.'

*   *   *

Some readers may be aware of the story of Nelson Rockefeller's son Michael, who vanished in 1961 while on an expedition to the Asmat region of Papua New Guinea. It was a worldwide news story at the time. He and his two colleagues were never found and, despite various claims, theories and investigations, the facts around his disappearance have always remained unclear, although the yacht that the Rockefeller group had been using had lost its mooring during a storm and was smashed on rocks, which provided a believable explanation why no bodies were ever found.

My visit to the country was only a few years afterwards, so the whole episode was not far from the front of my mind. I therefore took the opportunity to quiz my Patrol Officer about it. After some gentle persuasion, he asserted that the local Kiwai tribe of Nomad River had been responsible for killing Rockefeller and his colleagues.

According to the officer, Rockefeller had somehow generated a tribal fight between the Kiwai tribe and their neighbours, so that he could film the whole event. When the two tribes realized that they had been manipulated by 'the bad white men' in this way, they promptly killed and cannibalized them.

This outcome was apparently well known to the local police force, but to arrest and charge two whole tribes was no small undertaking. The Australian powers-that-be forced the whole thing to be hushed up, to avoid embarrassment, as one of the primary directives from the UN to the Australian administration at the time was to address the issue of cannibalism across the country.

* * *

During my time in Australia I also took the opportunity, along with some local colleagues, to visit East Timor, which in those days was still a Portuguese colony. We flew in from Darwin to Baucau, where we were surprised to be met by the local Governor, despite the fact that this was not an official visit.

I couldn't think why he was meeting us at the airstrip, nor why he was asking us if we had accommodation, until it transpired that our friendly Governor owned the only hotel in the small town. He helpfully ensured we got rooms, and we spent the evening in the hotel bar drinking with some Portuguese officers, until the Governor reappeared and asked us when we were intending going to bed.

'Er ... we're not sure, your Excellency ... why are you asking?'

'Because it's only when you have gone to bed that I can switch off the village generator.'

We spent a couple of days in Bacau. There was not a lot to do, although they did have a small beach. One morning after an overnight storm the beach was deserted, so I went for a quick dip. There were a few tree-trunks bobbing in the sea, which I presumed were there as a result of the storm. I was told afterwards that they were probably salt-water crocodiles, who had killed two locals only a few days earlier. Oops. Lucky escape.

With the beach out of action, there was not a lot to do in Bacau, so we rented a Land Rover and headed to the capital, Dili. On the way there, we discovered a wonderful beach just along the coast – beautiful sand, sparkling warm water, no logs or crocodiles to be seen, yet totally deserted. We spent a great afternoon sunning ourselves and swimming in the sea, our only company in the water being quite a large number of very pretty striped eels.

That evening, we got an invitation to dinner at the Australian consulate, where we enthused about our wonderful day at the nearby beach.

'Pity you've come at the wrong time of year for a dip, fellas – what with it being the breeding season for the local sea-snakes.'

'Ah – we thought we were swimming with colourful eels.'

Our host promptly choked on his beer.

'Swimming? Are you out of your minds? Those are Belcher sea-snakes, the most venomous snake in the world. I'm astonished none of you were killed!'

Apparently, the Belcher sea-snake's venom is ten times more lethal than that of a King Cobra. Oops again.

* * *

The single most memorable experience I had in Australia was in October 1966, during President Lyndon B. Johnson's visit to the region.

It was the first time a United States President had visited the country. Government House in Melbourne was chosen for one of the formal receptions due to the size of its ballroom – the grandest in Australia, deliberately designed to be 18 inches longer than the ballroom at Buckingham Palace. This visit was obviously a big deal for the Governor and all his staff, even though the primary purpose of the President's foreign trip was to meet in Manila with all his allies to promote his efforts to 'get it done or get out' in Vietnam.

Unfortunately, the Presidential visit to Government House got off to a bad start. We were all waiting for the President's motorcade to come up the drive, when it was ambushed at the gates by anti-war demonstrators demanding the withdrawal of Australian and US troops from Vietnam. They succeeded in covering the President's limo with red and green paint, the colours of choice in those early days of Vietnam War protests.

While the Governor and his wife met with the President and apologized for the local behaviour, I rushed down to the garage to see if we could clean up the limo. It would be a PR disaster if the President had to continue his journey through Melbourne with his Lincoln Continental displaying the colour scheme of the Vietcong flag.

Fortunately, Laurie Boyes, our head chauffeur and a wonderful chap, was already on the job. Laurie was an ex-middleweight boxing champion in the Australian Navy and had muscles on his muscles. I'm sure he was removing three coats of regular paint as well as the red and green stuff as he scrubbed away at the paintwork. Meanwhile, his teenage son Gary was making the most of this opportunity by taking photos of his Dad cleaning the United States President's limo.

On seeing Gary snapping away with his little camera, a burly American bodyguard strode over, grabbed him, snatched the camera out of his hand and opened it to expose and ruin the film.

'Kid – don't take photographs of the President's vehicle.'

Speaking those words was the last thing the bodyguard remembered for several minutes because, on seeing his son being taken to task in this way, Laurie promptly stepped up and knocked him out with a single right hook.

Chaos ensued. There were five different parties who thought they were in charge of the day's proceedings – the Australian State police, the Australian Federal police, the CIA, the U.S. Secret Service … .and my boss, the Governor. In the end, no action was taken against Laurie, mostly due to the common sense of Rufus Youngblood, who at the time was head of White House security. He was the secret service agent who, three years earlier at the assassination of President Kennedy, had thrown his body over Vice President Johnson to protect him as the shots were ringing out. He went on to become Deputy Director of the United States Security Service in 1969.

After all this excitement, I returned to the private part of the house, where the President was getting ready for the Federal Government reception. The Governor looked relieved.

'Mr President – my two ADCs, Captain Ritchie and Captain Hyde, will now escort you to the ballroom for the reception.'

We duly led the President and his entourage to a packed ballroom.

'Pray silence for the President of the United States of America!'

The national anthems were duly played, and then Captain Hyde and I set about the usual ADC routine for visiting dignitaries, which was to organize guests into groups of six.

'Hello, Sir, can I have your name, where you are from, and what you do?'

We would then lead the President to each group and introduce the individuals, while the other ADC organized the next group. It needed a good short-term memory for names and faces, which fortunately I had in my younger days.

'Mr President, may I have the honour to present Mr and Mrs A from X, where Mr A is the High School headmaster; Mr and Mrs B from Y where Mr B is Town Mayor; and Mr and Mrs C from Z, where they run the local brewery?'

After a few minutes of this process, the secret service chaps were getting itchy, and one of them strode up to me and complained loudly.

'Captain Ritchie, what the hell are you doing? This is the President of the United States of America, he does not get pushed around by a couple of British Army Captains!'

I was momentarily lost for words. Then the President spoke.

'No, I like the way the guys are doing this. From now on, I want to do it like this in the White House!'

We demurely blushed with pride.

Some considerable time later, after many introductions and much small talk, it was time for Captain Hyde and I to take the President back to the Governor's private rooms for dinner. It was then that we put our own plan into action.

We had learned from one of his staff on an early recce visit that the President was partial to Cutty Sark whisky. I had duly procured a bottle, which was waiting in our little shared office down a side corridor. As we walked with the President, with his entourage following, I made my play.

'Mr President, after such a busy reception, perhaps you would appreciate a quick Cutty Sark before dinner?'

His eyes lit up.

'You have Cutty Sark whisky?!'

'We do indeed, Mr President!'

We led President Johnson down the side corridor to our little office, where three glasses and a bottle of Cutty Sark Whisky were sat on my desk.

At my doorway, he turned to his security staff.

'You all wait here. This is just the Captains and me.'

And with that, the President of the United States closed the office door behind him, sat down in my chair, loosened his tie, put his feet up on my desk and enjoyed a very large glass of whisky with us, while his staff stood rather perplexed out in the corridor.

It was clear that the President was taking a much-needed breather and, for whatever reason, had taken a shine to the two young officers. I have met a few Texans in my time, and they do seem to have a particular affinity with us Scots. Maybe it goes all the way back to the Alamo, where the majority of Texans who fought and died were Scots-Irish or of direct Scottish descent.

After a couple of minutes, the Governor himself knocked and sheepishly put his head around the door.

'Er … Mr President … I see you have been ambushed by my ADCs.'

'Yes, I have, your Excellency. May I have another five minutes with them?'

The poor Governor winced and grudgingly withdrew. I refilled our glasses. It felt very unreal at the time, but we had to keep our wits about us. The President was asking us our views on Vietnam from a British perspective, and I didn't want to make rash promises to our American cousins about Britain being willing to offer support for their war.

All too soon, we had to rejoin the rest of the party for dinner, where Captain Hyde and I were seated well away from the President and the important guests. I thought that was an end to my time with arguably the most powerful person in the world. However, there was a little epilogue to the story …

The next morning, we were all on parade at the airport as the President prepared to leave on Air Force One. There were TV cameras everywhere and a long line of dignitaries who duly shook hands with the President as he made his way to the steps of the aircraft. I was stood on tiptoes in the line behind and felt rather deflated when I didn't manage to catch his eye.

Imagine my surprise, therefore – and that of everyone there that day, not to mention the thousands watching on live TV – when, at the top of the steps of Air Force One, having turned to give a quick wave, the President stopped. He then came back down the steps, walked over to the line of dignitaries, leaned in between the Governor and the Australian

Prime Minister and warmly shook the hand of an unknown young British Army Captain who was stood in full Royal Scots uniform.

'Captain Ritchie, I just spotted your Scottish hat from the steps. I just want to say thank you for last night – very enjoyable!'

And with that, and another wave to the crowd, he boarded the plane, leaving behind a very smug young ADC, an exasperated Governor and a very nonplussed Prime Minister.

*   *   *

Following the visit of President Johnson, the next state visit to Government House was by Air Marshal Ky, who at the time was the Prime Minister of South Vietnam. Air Marshal Ky had also planned this trip to garner support and credibility, both for his own position and for the war, which was intensifying in Vietnam.

His trip was perhaps a little undermined, unwittingly, by his being accompanied by his very attractive second wife. She was a 24-year-old ex-air-stewardess, who attracted a lot of press attention wherever the couple went. *Time* magazine had even run an article on her a few months earlier, when she had spent some time in a Tokyo hospital for unspecified 'cosmetic surgery'.

At dinner in Government House, I was delighted to find myself seated next to Madame Ky, with the Governor on her other side. Unlike her husband, Madame Ky did not speak any English, which made direct conversation with the Governor impossible. However, she spoke excellent French and, thanks to my Army language qualifications, my conversational French was decent. So for the early part of dinner, I translated for the Governor.

However, Madame Ky soon tired of the frustrating to-and-fro-ing of the translated small talk and, after I had deflected Air Marshal Ky's questioning about the British attitude to Vietnam and he had turned his attention to Lady Delacombe, the charming Madame Ky turned her full gaze to me and I found myself having a lovely chat with her in French, much to the Governor's frustration.

In fact, as we 'youngsters' chatted and giggled together, I could see the Governor getting more irate at my selfish behaviour. I was not doing my job of assisting the Governor but, to be fair, Madame Ky was *much* better looking than he. Finally, after an uncontrolled burst of laughter from yours truly, he snapped.

'What are you two finding so funny?'

'Well, Sir, er … I'd rather not say.'

That was tantamount to mutiny. I could be sent to the colonies – if I wasn't already there.

The Governor was bristling.

'I WANT TO KNOW WHAT YOU AND MADAME KY ARE TALKING ABOUT!'

His raised voice caused the dinner table to fall silent. I confess that I paused briefly for effect.

'Well, Sir, if you really must know – Madame Ky has been telling me about her new breast implants.'

* * *

The state visits of President Johnson and Air Marshal Ky were the most noteworthy events at Government House during my time as ADC. However, we did have many other very interesting people visit us, including such diverse characters as the RAF war hero Leonard Cheshire VC, the conductor and composer Sir Malcolm Sargent and, to my delight, the comic actor Tony Hancock.

Hancock had come to Melbourne as part of his touring review show. Perhaps his star was a little on the wane in the UK, but he was still a huge name, although stories of his increasing addiction to the demon drink did precede him.

Fortunately, the Governor and his wife happened to be away at the time. I tracked Hancock down to his hotel, got through to him on the phone, reminded him of when we had met and explained that I was now a Captain in the British Army and serving as an ADC to the Governor of Victoria. Would he like to come to Government House for lunch? I was delighted when he accepted.

He did drink quite a lot during lunch, taking advantage of the Governor's excellent cellar, and then spent some time sleeping it off by the private pool, before inviting me and a lady friend to attend as his guests at his review at the theatre in Melbourne, and then to dinner with him afterwards.

It became clear during dinner that the stories about his drinking were not exaggerated. He drank a prodigious amount of alcohol before firing a loaded question at me.

'Charles, do you think the Australians enjoyed my show tonight?'

I genuinely thought the show had been brilliant, but I didn't want to be obsequious, so I took a couple of seconds to gather my thoughts.

'Well, you could tell by the laughter that they absolutely loved you playing Tony Hancock of East Cheam. But when you were, for example, a Harbour Guide around Liverpool docks, well ... it seems they didn't find that *quite* as funny.'

Hancock immediately slammed his glass on the table, staggered to his feet, and in a very loud voice addressed the whole restaurant – most of whom had just been to the show.

'Don't you effing Australians understand? I'm not Hancock of East Cheam. There is NO character part I cannot play. I will defeat you Australians if it is the last thing I do!'

I thought at the time that, even taking the drink into account, it was a strange reaction and choice of words from a brilliant but very troubled man.

It was just two years later, when he returned to Australia for a TV series to be recorded in Sydney, that he committed suicide, aged just forty-four.

* * *

One of the big social events of the year in Melbourne is the Agricultural Show, when all the top estates across the state of Victoria display their best produce and animals.

I don't know about the present day, but back in the 1960s, on the night before the start of the show, the tradition was that all the young men known as the 'Cockies' would host a really good dinner party. On my second year in Melbourne, I wangled an invitation to it.

I drove to the party in a Government House car with a Crown number plate on it, which was naughty of me, but I wanted to arrive in style. I was conscious that I had to stay relatively sober and so I promised myself to stick to a modest amount of drink. I had a couple of glasses of wine before dinner, another couple during dinner, and a glass of port.

As I was leaving, a couple of Cockies stopped me.

'No, Charlie – before you leave, have a lager with us.'

I didn't want to offend and so I asked for a half-pint of lager from the barman. I sat with the Cockies while we drank and chatted, but when I then tried to leave, they would not have it.

'Hey, Charlie, you've only had half a pint! Bartender, fix our friend up with another half-pint.'

I duly drank the second half-pint of lager and then managed to make my escape. As I walked to the car I was surprisingly unsteady on my feet, but simply assumed I was overly tired.

Driving back into Melbourne along the main dual carriageway, I stopped at a set of traffic lights and a car pulled up alongside me. I remember thinking it would be a bit of fun to try to race it away from the lights. I put my foot down and got up to a speed of around 70mph in what was a 30mph zone, when my rival turned on its blue flashing light. Oops.

I managed to pull the car over reasonably gracefully, wound down my window and waited for the police officer to approach. To my great luck, he turned out to be Sergeant Don Quanchy, who organized all the police escorts when the Governor went on state occasions, opening of parliament, etc.

'Captain Ritchie! What the hell are you doing racing a police car?'

I was leaning on the open window of my car door trying to look nonchalant. Before I could think of a sensible reply, the Sergeant opened the door and I promptly fell into the road.

'My oath! You're as full as a bloody State School, you are!'

I did my best to try to explain what I had been doing, protesting that I really had not had that much to drink. Eventually, the good Sergeant bundled me into his car and drove me back to Government House, his fellow officer following behind with the Government House car.

The next day, I woke up with the most horrible of hangovers. I got a call around midday from the Sergeant.

'Charlie Ritchie – I've done some research on what happened to you last night. The barman at the club served you with two half-pints of lager, yes?'

'Yes, correct.'

'He's explained that, under the direction of a couple of Cockies, he put three measures of vodka in each of those lagers. You were set up, Charlie.'

The next day, I received a letter from the Chief Constable which I opened with some trepidation. If I was going to be prosecuted for drink-driving, I knew I would lose my job immediately.

Fortunately, the Sergeant's report had made it clear what had happened and so I was not charged, although the letter made it clear in no uncertain terms that I had to be on my best behaviour from then on. If I received a criminal record, I would have to leave Australia – ironic, I thought, given that it used to be a prerequisite for entry.

*   *   *

The Governor came to me one day in late January.

'Charles – we're going to have a big Burns Supper this year. You need to get hold of some haggis. Apparently, it's damned difficult to find in Australia.'

He wasn't kidding.

After much research and many phone calls, I eventually arranged for two dozen haggises to be delivered by the Navy, Army and Air Force Institute Shop in Singapore to the RAAF base there, then to be flown out to Melbourne on the next flight – just in time for the event.

On the morning of the Burns Supper, I received a welcome phone call from the Customs Office at the RAAF airbase in Melbourne.

'Captain Ritchie – I have two dozen haggises here for Government House with your name on them.'

'Great! I'll come and collect them.'

'Well, you can come – but I need to speak to you about these haggises.'

Thinking he might have some Scottish heritage and wanted to procure one for himself, I immediately drove down to the airbase, where I found the Customs officer. On his desk were the haggises.

'Captain Ritchie – we've got a problem here.'

'Oh yes? And what is that?'

'You can't import haggis into Australia. It does not meet our minimum requirements for the quality of foodstuffs. I can't release these for human consumption, they will have to be destroyed.'

We had something like fifty guests arriving that evening for a Burns Supper. How could it go ahead without any haggis? I protested, pleaded and prostrated myself.

After much discussion, the Customs Officer hit upon an idea. He drew up some labels, we signed some paperwork and I duly left with my two dozen haggises, labelled and signed for as 'agricultural fertiliser'.

* * *

At the end of my two-year stint working as an ADC, the Foreign Office paid for my trip home. I had the opportunity to make some stops and detours along the way, to visit various places I was keen to see for myself.

The first stop was Singapore, where the main event was an evening downtown hosted by the ADC for the local Governor who showed me the nightlife, including the cabaret shows of the 'ladyboys' of South-East Asia. Quite an experience.

I then flew to Hong Kong, where I stayed with John Charteris and his wife Antoinette. We had a great night downtown and woke up the next morning feeling very much the worse for wear. However, John was attached to the Army Air Corps as a helicopter pilot and had arranged to take me on a flight up to the Chinese border for a get-together with another old friend, Patrick Cardwell-Moore. Patrick was on attachment to the Gurkhas, deployed at one of the border posts due to the threat of invasion from Communist China.

Very hung over, John and I clambered into a Westland Scout helicopter, with my suitcase strapped to one of the landing struts. I did not have happy memories of flying in a Scout, but John somehow managed to get the chopper in the air, with my stomach trying to catch up.

As we flew north, it slowly dawned on me through an alcoholic haze that something didn't look right. We seemed to be flying on the wrong side of the very obvious border that ran between Communist China and Hong Kong. I looked across at my pilot, who had a fixed stare and hangover-induced beads of sweat on his face.

'Er ... John ... I think we may be flying in Communist China airspace.'
John seemed to have other things on his mind.

'Charles, I really don't care, as long as they have Alka-Seltzer.'

Somehow, we completed the journey without mishap. Given the political tensions during the latter half of that year, it would not have been a surprise – and they would have been totally within their rights –

if the Chinese had shot our helicopter out of the sky for invading their airspace.

We spent a few hours with Patrick, had a few drinks to settle our hangovers and then climbed back into the helicopter to head back. But as we took off, my suitcase decided it had had enough of being strapped to the outside of a chopper and dumped its contents all over the landing strip, the rotor blades scattering all my clothes.

Patrick kindly helped, by ordering his soldiers to help me recover my belongings, while he roared with laughter. We eventually set off, with the re-fastened suitcase lashed on the strut to within an inch of its life.

*   *   *

My next flight took me to Bangkok, where I stayed in an inexpensive little 3-star hotel. I confess my clearest memory is of boldly walking into one of the 5-star hotels on the riverside, nipping into the loo to change and then spending the rest of the day by their lovely private swimming pool.

I didn't need to try out that hotel scam in Calcutta, as members of the British Army could get a day pass to the very smart Calcutta Club and use their pool, which I did – although the two-page form I was asked to complete to get my day pass was the most detailed of its kind I have ever seen in my life. Who knows where and when their four grandparents were born? I certainly didn't and, unsurprisingly, the chap behind the admissions desk didn't either, so we had fun guessing.

There was a different kind of paperwork in Agra. I was on my way to see the Taj Mahal and the Agra Red Fort, but to get served a drink in the hotel the evening before, I had to apply in writing. The laws regarding alcohol consumption in India are pretty strict and differ from state to state. In that region at that time, they could only legally sell spirits to foreigners who were self-registered alcoholics.

'Great. Where do I sign?'

My visit to the Taj Mahal itself was absolutely fantastic. In those days it saw very few tourists, and there was not even a visitor's fee. The building looked absolutely magnificent, and I was able to stroll wherever I wanted, with hardly anyone else around. Down at the river there was a Hindu ceremony taking place, people bathing to wash away their sins. It was a very hushed and tranquil event, and so I watched from a distance, spellbound. In the late afternoon I even sat in front of the Taj Mahal on the same centrally positioned marble seat as did Diana the Princess of Wales for that iconic photo during her visit, 25 years later.

* * *

My next port of call was Kabul. I knew very little about Afghanistan but was keen to visit the Khyber Pass, due to its long military history, including its role in three Anglo-Afghan wars. On the plane from New Delhi to Kabul I met up with an American who was also keen to visit the Pass, so we agreed to team up.

However, on disembarking from the plane I was met by a driver from the British Embassy, who had been ordered to take me to see the Defence Attaché. I wasn't particularly surprised by this, as the Foreign Office had sent a copy of my itinerary to all Embassies and High Commissions on my route. I collected my suitcase and was duly driven to the British Embassy in Kabul, where I was met by a very grumpy Colonel Trimbell.

'Captain Ritchie – what the hell are you doing in Kabul? Don't you know that Afghanistan is out of bounds to all members of the British Armed Forces?!'

'Er … no, Sir, I was not aware of that.'

'Well, you bloody well should have been.'

I explained my desire to visit the Khyber Pass and, with some trepidation, the Colonel gave me the okay, as well as some personal advice for the trip.

'Listen here, Ritchie – Afghanistan is *not* a country – it never *has* been a country and it never *will* be. Once you are 30 miles out of Kabul you are in lawless tribal areas. Take a roll of dollar bills with you, and hand one over at each road-block you come across.'

I made my way to the hotel to check in and rejoin my new American friend. We planned our trip for the next day, arranged a taxi and driver and sorted out our rolls of dollar bills.

The journey itself was much as the Colonel had described. We went through various road-blocks, where threatening-looking tribesmen, armed to the teeth, happily took our US dollars in exchange for safe passage. We spent an hour or so taking photographs of the Pass. The whole day was remarkably uneventful.

That evening, back in Kabul, we were heading off to a restaurant for something to eat, when I was stopped by a very attractive, well-spoken young woman.

'I'm sorry but ... you look British?'

'Yes, indeed I am, and my friend here is American.'

'Oh, thank God for that ...'

She claimed she had arrived in Kabul in a minibus with a girlfriend and four young men – basically on the 'hippie trail' that had evolved in those days, and on which Kabul was a major stop en route. The men had sold the minibus to buy drugs, and now she had no money and no way to get home.

I was obviously suspicious of such a sorry tale. But the girl was clearly very distressed and seemed genuine, so we took her to get something to eat while we heard more of her story. She explained where she lived in the UK, where she had gone to school, what her father did, etc., and I concluded by the end of dinner that she was indeed genuine and in trouble.

I gave her some local currency –the equivalent of about £40 sterling – and she gave me the address of her parents, with a request that I contact them when I got to London, which I duly did. They were very relieved to get a phone call from me to say that their daughter was safe, as they had lost all contact with her for over a month. I explained to them how to wire money to the British Consul in Kabul to enable her to get home. I never did meet her again, but her father sent me £200 as a thank you, which was immensely kind of him.

* * *

I then flew to Baghdad, as I wanted to see the site of the Hanging Gardens of Babylon. On arrival at immigration, I was immediately arrested and taken to a cell at the side of the airport. Unknown to me, my visa, which I had got from the Iraqi Affairs section of the Egyptian Embassy in Canberra, had written on it in Arabic 'Captain CDM Ritchie, British Army'.

I had been in the cell for about an hour when the door opened and an Iraqi Army Major entered, speaking faultless English.

'You say you are a Captain in the British Army. Well, I was at Sandhurst myself, so I will be able to tell if you are lying.'

He then proceeded to bombard me with all sorts of questions that only someone who had been to Sandhurst would know the answer to, like 'Where is the statue of Queen Victoria?' Once he was satisfied he sent me on my way, but it soon became obvious that I was being tailed.

After checking into my hotel I went for a stroll, closely followed by my 'shadow'. Baghdad in those days was beautiful – lovely cafes, bars and restaurants – and I entered a cinema that was showing a Western. The chap behind the ticket counter spoke English, so with a smile I bought two tickets and asked him to give the second one to my 'shadow', who dutifully sat two rows behind me.

Next day, I was told by the concierge at the hotel to get a No. 7 bus to the museum and then find a bus to Hillah. As I left the hotel, a No. 7 bus, which was, amazingly, a London double-decker 'Routemaster', was just pulling away. I sprinted after it and hopped on the open platform at the back. Then, remembering my 'shadow', I turned around to give him a wave goodbye, which was warmly reciprocated with a shake of his fist.

On reaching the museum stop, I discovered a mass of minibuses but eventually found one that was about to head south to Hillah. It was a slow journey, through several road-blocks, but eventually we got to Hillah and I was dropped off close to the entry to the ruins, where I found a sleeping sentry at the gate. I pointed behind him.

'Shufti?'

He picked up an old telephone handset and made a call. A minute later, an excitable chap appeared and introduced himself in perfect English as the Director of Antiquities at Babylon. He was overjoyed to see me.

'You're the first tourist we have had in a long time!'

He was a charming fellow and proceeded to give me a personal tour around the ruins, which was thoroughly enjoyable. At the end of the tour, aware that a financial tip would be frowned upon, I gave him a box of Benson & Hedges cigarettes that I had planned to take home with me, by way of thanks for his hospitality. He was delighted, exclaiming that he hadn't had a Benson & Hedges cigarette for ten years, and we departed the best of friends.

When I got back to the hotel in Baghdad, I was promptly arrested again.

'Where have you been all day?'

I explained exactly where I had been and gave the name of the Director of Antiquities at Babylon. A call was made, and my new-found friend was only too happy to confirm my story.

However, I was clearly *persona non grata* in Baghdad, so I left the next morning. As our commercial flight taxied from the terminal to the runway, I noticed a massive line of Iraqi Air Force jets. I took a whole roll of 'holiday snaps' with my camera out of the plane window, which the Intelligence chaps back in London greatly appreciated.

*   *   *

The flight from Baghdad was a short hop west to Beirut. In those days, like Baghdad, it was a very pleasant place to visit, with Muslims and Christians seemingly living happily side by side. I stayed for a couple of days at the St George's Club on the harbour, another private members' club that offered temporary membership to British officers, and took the opportunity to visit the amazing Roman ruins at Baalbek.

My last evening in Beirut was due to be my last few hours of leisure on the trip home, with only an overnight stay in Istanbul before arriving in London. I was delighted, therefore, to accept the invitation of a fellow resident of the St George's Club to share a taxi to the Beirut Casino. Why not blow the last of my cash on one final night out?

We enjoyed a wonderful dinner and a spectacular floor show, including the very bizarre spectacle of naked female swimmers in an underfloor pool, viewed only via a huge mirror angled below the stage.

Several years in the Army had already taught me that I was dangerously useless at card games, so in the casino I wandered up to one of the roulette tables to use up the last of my spare cash – the grand sum of fifty US dollars.

Despite betting very modestly, I was quickly down to my last $10 of chips. So, with a final flourish, I placed them all on my lucky number 17… and lo and behold, the little silver ball landed on it! With congratulatory pats on the back from my fellow gamblers, I immediately took my $350 worth of chips to get cashed at the desk, delighted to be going home with a decent sum of money to tide me over until my Army paychecks started up again.

While the cashier was still counting out my winnings, there were yells from the roulette table I had been at. I looked over to see that everyone was frantically waving to me. I had not retrieved my original $10 bet from number 17, it had been left there by the croupier for the next spin of the wheel – and 17 had come up a second time in a row! Another $350 came my way, the croupier got a healthy tip and the drinks were on me back at the St George's Club.

Chapter 7

Such Stuff as Schemes are Made on

Following my ADC stint in Australia, my next posting was a two-year spell as the Adjutant for the 52nd Lowland Volunteers, a Territorial Army Regiment based in Glasgow.

I arrived to take up my new role on 16 January 1968. It was the day after one of the worst storms ever to have hit Scotland, which claimed twenty lives, damaged tens of thousands of homes, sank ships in the River Clyde and caused general chaos. The streets of Glasgow were littered with masonry and debris, and there was a power cut across the city. I had already been in a few battle-zones in my short career, but this was quite extraordinary. Many compared the damage to that of the Nazi blitz on Clydebank in 1941.

I slowly picked my way through the debris in the streets to reach the Regimental HQ on Hotspur Street in the Maryhill area of Glasgow. On arrival, I found the entrance cordoned off by the police. The doorway had been the scene of a murder only hours before.

That was quite an introduction to life in Glasgow.

* * *

I had an early taste of the local culture whilst spending a Sunday evening at my desk catching up on some work. There were a few chaps in the regimental bar which, unlike all the civilian pubs in the city in those days, was able to stay open on a Sunday evening. This gave the TA soldiers a chance to have a drink together, before returning home to prepare for their 'day jobs' on Monday morning.

The sound of raised voices came down the corridor and disturbed me from my paperwork.

'Wha' the f*** d'ya mean, I canna come in?'

'That's the rule, Sir.'

'Sez who?!'

'Says our Adjutant, Captain Ritchie.'

'Who the f*** is this Captain Ritchie?'

By this point I had walked down the corridor to the entrance and so introduced myself in person.

'Hello – I am Captain Ritchie.'

'Well – d'ya ken who ah am? Ah'm Jimmy McDoug, of the Maryhill Fleet.'

I had no idea that 'Maryhill Fleet' was the name of the most notorious 'razor gang' in Glasgow. Instead, picking out the word 'fleet' from the broad Glaswegian accent, I tried to be helpful.

'Ah well, Sir, if you are a member of the Royal Naval Reserve, you are very welcome here …'

I sensed the soldier next to me shrink into his boots. The two 'heavies' accompanying Mr McDoug began to salivate in anticipation, as their boss became even more agitated.

'So … a funny man, eh?'

'Well, I …'

'Listen, pal … awa' tae the lavvy and hae a last look at yer face in the mirror … cos it'll no' be looking like that ever again.'

It dawned on me that I was under threat, so I brought out the Company Sergeant Major, who managed to placate Mr McDoug and send him on his way. The Sergeant Major then drove me home that evening just in case, although I never crossed paths with Jimmy McDoug again. Nor did he ever again try to use our Regimental bar as his Sunday evening hostelry.

*   *   *

I spent two years as the TA Adjutant in Glasgow and enjoyed it thoroughly. It was, however, hard work, and I had very little free time, particularly as weekends were usually busy with TA volunteers on exercise. Even on my rare weekends off, I was often roped into some additional task or other.

One of the various Cadet Force units was stationed in Hotspur Street, and the Cadet Officer was a school teacher who always seemed rather over-stretched. He poured his heart out to me one evening over a quick drink.

'Charles, I've an awful problem. I take the Cadets out every other weekend, we do gym nights every Tuesday and we have our military night every Thursday. When I add all that to all my school-teaching responsibilities, I'm hardly ever at home.'

'Is that a problem?'

'Well, my wife has given me an ultimatum – it's either her or the Cadets.'

I had met his wife and, to me, the decision was an obvious one.

However, in a rare moment of gallantry, I bit my tongue. But in terms of helping the poor fellow, the Army was responsible for providing the facilities for the Cadets, but not manpower. So I offered my sympathies, but nothing more.

The very next day, I got a phone call telling me that the Cadets' Captain had resigned from his role, two days before the Cadets were due to go on a weekend camp. It was explained to me that nothing had been organized, but we couldn't let the youngsters down, not good PR for the Army, etc. Would I please organize and run the weekend camp?

It was due to be one of my rare weekends off and I had an invitation to a big party on Friday evening in Edinburgh, so I roped in one of our Sergeants to help. We made a few quick phone calls to set a few things up and on Friday afternoon we bundled a dozen teenage lads and a load of camping gear into a 4-ton army truck. The Sergeant then followed me, as I drove the Land Rover to my parents' property in the countryside outside Edinburgh. The tents were pitched in a nearby field, and I left the good Sergeant to feed and water the cadets while I changed into my dancing shoes and drove off to town.

I can't recall any details about the party itself, so it must have been a jolly good one. But I distinctly remember driving back to my parents' house at around 3.00am. It was midsummer, one of those quite beautiful Scottish summer mornings when the first light of dawn is already appearing, the birds are already awake and there are sweet sounds and smells on the air. As I slowly made my way up the drive, full of the joys, I bade good morning to a rabbit calmly munching by the roadside, nodded acknowledgement to a swallow as it swept across my bonnet – and then nearly flattened a semi-naked boy as he stumbled out in front of me.

Before I had time to get out of the car, several other cadets appeared in varying degrees of undress. I quickly rounded them up, got them back to their tents and enquired about the early-morning rambling. After much shuffling of dirty feet and embarrassed wiping of noses, they explained that they had never been out of the city of Glasgow in their lives, and the noises of the countryside had kept them scared and awake most of the night.

I managed to catch a couple of hours' sleep myself, and then the Sergeant and I spent the day entertaining the cadets. Fortunately, I had managed to rope in a neighbouring landowner who was very generous with his time. He gave the boys a grand tour around his farm, showed the cows being milked, demonstrated shearing a sheep, took them fishing and even let them try out his shotguns. He then finished the day with a barbecue – what a chap!

That night, the boys all slept very soundly, and on Sunday we did a brief cross-country trek to round off the weekend, before packing up and heading back to Glasgow, mission accomplished.

*   *   *

It was always important to give the TA volunteers training exercises that were as realistic as possible. For one battlefield simulation we decided to mount a night attack exercise at the Barry Buddon training centre near Carnoustie in Fife.

I had got a chap called Keith Steele to supply me with a couple of old 'Bangalore Torpedoes' – specialist mine- and wire-clearing explosive devices left over from the Second World War. The Bangalore was invented by a Captain of the Royal Engineers while attached to the Indian Army in 1912, as a way to detonate booby traps and demolish barricades. They were not exactly modern in design.

The Training Major, Alistair Thorn, agreed to my plan for the night exercise, which was to detonate the Bangalores ahead of the attacking troops, to simulate a real-world attack scenario. I did not confess that I had never come across these explosives before, but I knew roughly how they were used, so what was the worst that could happen?

We deployed a run of barbed wire and set the detonators to explode at exactly 2200 hours, when the attack was due to set off from the 'start line' a few hundred yards away. We then departed the scene and monitored the countdown to the start of the exercise from the edge of the training grounds a couple of miles away. I was fascinated by explosives of all types and was looking forward to seeing how Keith's old Bangalores would perform.

Imagine my dismay when my watch ticked past 2200 without the Bangalores detonating. Damn! Grabbing my radio, I yelled to the officer commanding the simulated attack.

'Alpha One, Alpha One – stop the exercise, the Bangalores have not gone off.'

Silence. In a classic double-whammy that the British Army is superbly expert at, the radio battery was also dead.

We had no way to stop the soldiers, who were presumably already merrily charging towards the barbed wire and unexploded ordnance. It would only take them a couple of minutes to reach the wire – but as I was still desperately working through the options of what to do, there was an almighty explosion as the Bangalores went off just in time, with such massive force that it caught everyone by surprise. The ground shook, shrapnel flew through the air, all the locals within a five-mile radius fell out of bed, and no doubt some geologists from Dundee University got terribly excited.

Fortunately, no one was injured. The part-time soldiers, bless them, continued their charge through the smoke towards what was left of the wire with their ears ringing, only to discover that they now had to manoeuvre across a massive crater instead.

My meeting the next morning with the Company Commander was brief and to the point.

'Charles, are you suffering from insanity?'

'I don't suffer, Sir – I quite enjoy it.'

'I will never ask you to organize a battlefield simulation again.'

'Very good, Sir.'

*   *   *

While in Glasgow I got re-acquainted with an old school friend, Tim Boycott, who had joined the Royal Navy. Tim happened to be stationed briefly at the Clyde shipyards, supervising some armaments being installed on a naval destroyer, so we spent a bit of time together, which was great fun.

A tarts and vicars party was organized one weekend by some friends, which Tim and I decided we would attend as 'Monks with Guns'. We hired some monks' robes, bought two plastic imitation pistols, got ourselves dressed up and set off to the party in his sports car.

On the way, we stopped to buy a couple of bottles of wine in an area of Glasgow I wasn't very familiar with. I nipped into the off-licence, in full monk regalia, and the charming shop-owner enquired as to my fashion sense and where I was heading. I enthusiastically gave him all the details of the tarts and vicars party before completing my purchase but, as I turned to leave, a young boy of about ten stood boldly in front of me.

'We dinnae like yooz Roman Caflicks in oor street – this is a Pro'stant street.'

Eyeing up my runny-nosed adversary, I decided to play the tough monk. I pulled out my plastic pistol and pointed it between his eyes.

'Another religious remark like that, sonny, and I'll blow your head off.'

With that, I exited the shop, hopped into Tim's car, and the Monks with Guns roared off along the streets of Glasgow.

Just as we were reaching our destination, we heard an urgent police siren wailing behind us. We pulled over. The police car stopped in front of us and two of Strathclyde's finest stepped out. One stayed by the car, while the other approached us.

I guess it's not every day that a Strathclyde bobby pulls over two monks in a sports car but, to give him his due, he did not raise an eyebrow.

'Did wan o' yooz gentlemen have an altercation wi' a wee laddie in an offie jist now?'

'Ah, that would have been me, officer. Cheeky little blighter was having a go at my outfit.'

'Oh aye? But did ye threaten to shoot the wee lad?'

Wow. News travels fast in this part of Glasgow, I thought. Perhaps the boy was the shop-owner's son. How else could the police have known where we were going?

In situations like this, the best course of action is to whip out your military ID. All the uniformed services have a grudging respect for each other, even if in this case the uniforms were a little unorthodox.

Tim and I handed over our Navy and Army identity badges with cool and knowing smiles, expecting to be waved on our way. To our dismay, however, the opposite occurred. Our alert Strathclyde officer, armed with nothing more than his trusty truncheon, clearly thought that he had two liquored-up military nutters on his hands, armed to the teeth and willing to take on all-comers, children included.

He motioned to his partner to join him, while his tone to us immediately changed to one of nervous action.

'Both o' ye – hands oan the dashboard wher' I can see 'em!'

There followed a rather embarrassing question-and-answer session, before we were permitted to draw out our toy pistols to demonstrate that we were nothing more than two fun-loving young officers with an evening of innocent, if rather ribald, revelry on our minds.

We were eventually sent on our way, with a firm recommendation to lock our toys in the car and not try anything so stupid with the locals ever again. Suitably chastised, we complied.

* * *

The two years I spent in Glasgow happened to coincide with the emergence of one of the city's great characters – Billy Connolly, now a knight of the realm, of course. He was at the start of his career in the late 1960s, playing folk music in local clubs with Gerry Rafferty, his comedy limited to the banter between songs.

Billy was a Sergeant in the Territorial Army at the time – the 15th Scottish Battalion, the Parachute Regiment, to be precise. He was a really charming young man, who was easy to get on with, immensely popular and obviously incredibly funny and entertaining. After one of his gigs on Sauchiehall Street that we all attended, he threw a party for all members of the Sergeants' Mess and Officers' Mess, which was when I first met him in person.

Our paths crossed again many years later, at Heathrow Airport of all places, when he was kind enough to claim to remember me. We got chatting, and I explained to him that I had just come back from South Africa, where I described to him a lucky escape I had had while driving in a storm …

I was just about to drive through a small tunnel under the railway line when there was a blinding flash and an explosion. I thought our car had been hit by an RPG (Rocket-Propelled Grenade) so I free-wheeled down into the tunnel for protection, with the car still crackling and fizzing. I jumped out, to find that the car's roof had been struck by lightning.

Fortunately, everyone in the car was unhurt other than being temporarily blinded by the flash, and the car was still serviceable, although clearly damaged. However, when we got back to the airport at Johannesburg to hand our car in, the rental chap made a terrible fuss about the cost of the damage.

I refused to pay up, which got him even more agitated. Apparently, after some more arguing and ever-increasing hostility, he claimed that we were not covered by insurance because a lightning strike was considered by the rental company as 'an Act of God'.

I then came out with possibly the only clever thing I've ever said in my life.

> 'If this is an Act of God, then please get in touch with the Archbishop of Johannesburg. He is God's senior representative here, and if God has done this to the car then you should ask the Church for compensation.'

We were sent on our way with nothing to pay.

Billy howled with laughter at this story. He had had his own well-documented run-ins with religious bodies during his career and asked if he could potentially use the story.

I then forgot all about it until many years later, when a film came out called *The Man Who Sued God*, in which Billy plays a fisherman whose boat is struck by lightning and sinks. He is then told he is not insured as it was an Act of God, so he takes all the Churches to court and – spoiler alert - wins his case.

Sadly, I never met Billy again and I didn't get an invite to the film's opening night!

* * *

My first tour of Northern Ireland was in the role of Battalion Public Relations Officer, based at Springfield Road's Royal Ulster Constabulary (RUC) Station in Belfast.

There is really no such thing as a formal Battalion Public Relations Officer. I was given the task purely because I joined the battalion in the middle of a tour, so they could not immediately give me an operational role as I had not done the reconnaissance and therefore did not have the necessary experience or knowledge on the ground.

Therefore, the job was created to give me something to do, alongside standard stuff such as being the Duty Officer in the Ops room. As a result, any time the press appeared, I was the one to deal with them. It may seem to have been a strange job for someone a lady friend once described at a dinner party as having the tact and diplomacy of a brick. At least, I think she said the word 'brick'; it was hard to hear over all the tutting.

*   *   *

The Magnet Youth Club was a very successful venture run by the British Army, right on the boundary of the Lower Falls, which separated the Protestant and Catholic communities. The Club was in a building that had a door on one side for the Protestant kids to come and go, and another door on the other side for the Catholic kids. In the club itself, they mixed together happily.

The success of the Club reached the ears of the BBC's *Panorama* programme, who decided they wanted to do a piece about it. They approached us for permission, and I requested a go-ahead from our PR people who, in their infinite wisdom, asked that the programme be prefixed by an interview with our Commanding Officer, so that he could expound to camera his overall policy and views. I duly explained to the BBC that this was what the Army wanted, but they were not at all happy about the interference with their creative flow.

'This is an independent piece. We don't want to interview your CO. We just want it to be about Protestant and Catholic kids playing together, we're not interested in what some Brigadier or Colonel has to say.'

I was very keen for the piece to be done but was caught between a rock and a hard place. I decided a little bit of creativity of my own was required.

'Tell you what – interview my CO in advance, to keep him happy. You don't have to include the interview clip when the programme goes out on air.'

The CO was duly interviewed, and I naively hoped that he might then forget all about it. However, the programme was scheduled for the very next week, which meant he quickly got rather excited about seeing himself on national TV.

I could sense that my actions were about to backfire on me, so I managed to rope in some colleagues to ensure that, just before the programme was due to start, they manufactured a false alarm that took the CO away to the Operations Room. By the time he returned, the programme had finished.

'Damn. Was it any good?'

'Er ... yes, Sir, very good.'

'Was I on? How was that bit?'

'Er ... I think they had to cut quite a lot of your bit, Sir.'

Thank goodness the VCR had not yet been invented.

* * *

Panorama also did a piece, a few months later, on how British troops deployed on UK soil were receiving a Campaign Service Medal for performing homeland security duties. The BBC wanted to interview someone from the Army who had also served in campaigns abroad. Due to my time in Aden and the Yemen and my role as a PR Officer in Belfast, they assumed that I was the obvious choice. My CO reluctantly agreed.

And so I appeared on prime time UK TV, and in some newspapers, saying roughly the following:

> Quite honestly, I don't think we should be awarded a Service Medal for this operation. I joined the British Army to serve abroad and to defend it from external aggression. I don't want a medal for serving on the streets of the United Kingdom.

I obviously should not have been challenging the heads of the Army in this way. The Army Board went ballistic, and I was duly carpeted by the Brigadier, who had been ordered by General Sir Ian Freeland of the Royal Anglian Regiment, Commander-in-Chief of the British Army in Northern Ireland, to give me the most imperial bollocking.

* * *

Thankfully, I went some way to restoring my credibility when I was with my PR photographer on the Springfield Road during some terrible rioting. A Protestant march had come down off the Shankhill Road and paraded up to a housing estate which was predominantly Catholic. A major riot ensued.

The Army had attempted to block off access to the rioters but, unknown to us, they had been getting around the blockade by nipping in the back doors of houses and out by the front doors into the next street.

While the rioting was in full swing, I caught sight of two men in a doorway attacking someone. I rushed up, drew my pistol and yelled something inarticulate at the top of my voice, at which point they fortunately scarpered, leaving the individual shaken but otherwise not badly injured. As I helped him away, I realized it was none other than Martin Bell, who was the BBC's chief correspondent in Northern Ireland at the time.

* * *

I had a bizarre experience while observing a road-block operation on a day of lashing rain and freezing cold. We had stopped a couple in their car who unfortunately had a very unhappy baby in the back seat, crying its little heart out. We had an RUC officer with us who suspected that something more serious was awry – she spotted that the baby was lying very high in a carry-cot, almost rolling out of the top.

We asked the couple in the car to step out, which they did. They were very polite and charming, commiserating with us that we were out in such filthy weather. But when we went to lift the baby's carrycot, they both went ballistic, screaming obscenities at us to leave their baby alone.

While the parents were restrained, we carefully picked up the crying baby and found the reason for its discomfort. It was lying on several automatic pistols and hundreds of rounds of ammunition, destined to be delivered to the IRA.

* * *

To generate some positive PR for The Royal Scots, we occasionally had to show some creativity.

One example was when we borrowed a local woman's dog and its three new-born pups. We put the dogs on a blanket in a sentry box on the Peace Line and got the local press along to take photos. This was then reported as The Royal Scots finding a stray dog and kindly letting her deliver her pups in a sentry box.

On another occasion, we got pictures published of a very attractive young woman delivering books to the poor bored British squaddies. For some added fun, she agreed to be pictured accidentally dropping the books in shy embarrassment.

The stunt that got the best reaction was more straightforward. We dressed up a very keen six-year old lad in uniform, with his mum's permission, and he stood to attention for photo opportunities in a sentry box outside Battalion HQ.

*   *   *

Everyone from the press used to gather in McGlades Bar. I was there one evening and got chatting to a very charming girl who worked for the *Irish News*. We had quite a lot to drink and, at the end of the evening, I offered to escort her home. She ordered a taxi, which duly arrived, and we hopped in.

It was only then that it dawned on me that I might be in a spot of bother. We were in a black cab, which we were forbidden to use as it was believed many were run by IRA activists or sympathizers. Worse still, when the girl gave her home address to the driver, I realized she lived in the Lower Falls. This was an extreme no-go area for us, as it was an IRA stronghold behind barricades.

We passed through the IRA road-block without fuss, with the girl doing the talking. By then I was sobering up quickly, as it dawned on me that all it needed was for this girl to state that she was with a British Army officer dressed in civvies, and I would have been killed – no question.

The taxi dropped us off outside her house, and when it was time to say goodnight, she gave me instructions on how to get out of the Lower Falls on foot. This included acting as nonchalantly as I could when walking right past the IRA barricades with a casual wave, as she assured me that no one paid any attention to someone *leaving* the Lower Falls.

As I walked back up towards Springfield Road I could hear sirens and commotion, and emerging on to the main road, I found myself next to a taxi office that had just been petrol-bombed. There were police and Army units everywhere, and I was met by Major Dudley Lucas.

'Captain Ritchie – what the hell have you been doing?'

I gave a rather evasive reply and was led back to the police station for safety. The next day, Major Lucas complained to my Commanding Officer about my suspicious appearance from the Lower Falls.

Fortunately, despite my stupidity at risking my life in such a way, my CO stood up for me and stated for the record that I had been 'on a special Public Relations mission'. Indeed, my relations had never been so public.

Chapter 8

Is this an AK47 I See Before Me?

From 1972 to 1974 I was back at RMA Sandhurst, this time as an instructor. I taught 'Intake 52', which was the last Sandhurst intake to enjoy a full two-year officer training course. All courses from then on were reduced to just six months, with the majority of the academic subjects being dropped – a change which I personally have always thought was a bad idea.

* * *

One of my best students was Officer Cadet Ian Khama. I knew nothing of his background until I received unusual orders one day from my CO.

'Ritchie – got any plans for Saturday?'

'Yes, Sir – I am going to a party in Norfolk.'

'No, you're not – you're having lunch with the President of Botswana and his wife, at the Hyde Park Hotel in London. The President wants to discuss how his son Ian is doing at Sandhurst. This is high profile, Ritchie – don't muck it up.'

It suddenly dawned on me that Officer Cadet Ian Khama was the son of the famous couple, Sir Seretse Khama and Ruth Williams, whose marriage had been the cause of great consternation and political nonsense at the time. An excellent film was recently made of their story – *A United Kingdom*, starring David Oyelowo and Rosamund Pike.

I duly met Sir Seretse and his wife for lunch. They were both utterly charming and engaging, but after some small talk we had to get down to business. Fortunately, I was able to give the couple a very positive report on their son's progress. The President was pleased to hear the news, but then made his position clear.

'Captain Ritchie – I am really relying on you.'

'In what sense, Mr President?'

'It is Ian's destiny to follow me and to be elected President of Botswana one day. I am expecting you to give him a thorough education and teach him properly.'

That marked my card.

I never met Sir Seretse again, and he sadly died a few years later. However, I did stay in touch with his son Ian once he was commissioned. He went on to become Major General of the Botswana Defence Force, before retiring from the military and entering politics. He served as acting President for an interim period before a formal Presidential election was held in 2009.

He came to visit me just before that election. It was only then that I sat him down and told him the story of my lunch meeting with his parents all those years previously and what his father had said to me about his son's destiny. Ian was, as you can imagine, very taken aback.

'I had better win this bloody election, then.'

He did.

* * *

Colonel Jim Alexander, the College Commander, called me to his office one morning, which was a surprise, as I hadn't put my foot in anything for quite a few days.

'Ritchie – you've done a tour in Northern Ireland, right?'

'Yes, Sir.'

'Right – on my desk by Monday morning, I want plans for a road-block exercise, a riot control exercise, and a cordon-and-search exercise.'

'Very good, Sir.'

I duly planned the exercises. We set up multiple road-blocks around the grounds, with a different platoon of cadets assigned to each, and had instructors and their wives and children roped in to play 'clean' or 'dirty' members of the public, the latter having some form of weapon or ammunition hidden about their person or in their vehicle.

On the day of the exercises, the Colonel appeared in my office. Princess Anne and Captain Mark Phillips had recently moved to Sandhurst, and he was clearly agitated.

'Ritchie – is *you-know-who* taking part in your exercises today?'

'No, Sir – but all the other wives are.'

'Very good – carry on.'

Five minutes after the Colonel had left, Mark came storming in.

'Charles – you never told me all the wives were taking part in this exercise!'

'Well, come on Mark … surely … it's not appropriate …?'

That was the wrong thing to say.

'Charles – am I not a Captain Instructor here?'

'Yes.'

'Am I married with a wife living here?'

'Yes.'

'Well, then. Anne will love doing this sort of thing. Let me use your phone.'

Mark called the Princess, they had a quick chat, and then he turned back to me.

'She's on her way over now.'

Mark went off to look after his platoon of Officer Cadets and I went to meet the Princess when she arrived in her Reliant Scimitar. It was a very striking vehicle, registration number 1420 H, as she was at the time Colonel-in-Chief of the 14th/20th Hussars.

I explained that I would like her to drive her car in the road-block exercise, acting as a 'dirty'. I proceeded to place an AK47 assault rifle on the back seat under the dog blanket, which her dog Pleasure then lay on top of, as well as a dummy hand grenade in the glove compartment and some ammunition in the engine bay.

I then met up with Mark, who was watching his platoon from Chapel Hill while they were stationed at the first road-block. Mark had already briefed his platoon to 'take this exercise very seriously, no matter who you are met by, and that includes my mother-in-law', which got an appreciative laugh from his cadets.

Nevertheless, they were clearly surprised when his wife drove up to their road-block. She played her part beautifully. As the cadets approached, she wound down her window and shouted at them.

'What's going on here? I've got some urgent business to attend to, let me through!'

Before the cadets could react, the Colonel arrived on the scene, saw the Princess shouting from her car and ran up to the road-block, yelling at the cadets.

'Clear the road now! Move everything out of the way!'

He then turned sharply to the car and snapped a salute.

'Your Royal Highness, I do apologize. I will have you on your way in just a moment.'

The Princess was obviously not happy that her involvement in the exercise was being compromised in such a way.

'I'm very sorry, I don't know who you are, but will you please stop ruining Charles Ritchie's exercise?'

The Colonel turned red, stepped back and yelled at the top of his voice.

'Ritchie – when I find you, I'm going to kill you!'

He then stormed off, leaving Mark's cadets to search the Princess's car. They made a quick check of the back seat but did not move the dog, so did not find the gun. They briefly opened the glove compartment but did not root down to the bottom to find the grenade. And they opened the bonnet but did not spot the ammunition strapped to the side wall.

I avoided the Colonel for the rest of the day, but he caught up with me the next morning, still seething.

'Ritchie – I've never been so humiliated or embarrassed in my life! You explicitly told me that the Princess was not taking part in the exercise!'

'I know, Sir, and when I told you that, it was true. But she turned up a short time later, very keen to take part, and I had no time to let you know …'

As it happens, he did not discipline me, because using the Princess in the exercise had been a very good lesson for the cadets. In all, as she proceeded through each of the road-blocks, only two of the six cadet platoons successfully found the items hidden in her car. The others had clearly been distracted by who she was and had not followed their orders to the letter, which in a real situation could have cost lives.

* * *

The final exercise on the Officer Cadet course before cadets were commissioned was always a week-long event abroad. Our intake went to Cyprus, which had – and still has – a major British military presence.

At the time, tensions between the Greeks and Turks on the island were high. The military coup that triggered the Turkish invasion of Cyprus was to happen only a few months later, and there was already a fair degree of cross-border shenanigans going on.

We held a cadet briefing in Sandhurst the day before our departure, which included a Q&A session with Major Robert Gurdon of The Black Watch regarding safety and the like, particularly with regard to the political tensions. The final question from the cadets, however, involved the local fauna.

'Sir – are there any snakes in Cyprus?'

The Major's answer was unequivocal.

'Absolutely not – *there are no snakes in Cyprus.*'

Armed with that comforting thought, the officer cadets were dismissed to get their kit packed.

On the first day's exercise in Cyprus, we were marching the cadets along a path when there was a cry from the front of the column.

'Sir, Sir – there's a snake in the middle of the path in front of us.'

'There can't be! What did Major Gurdon say just the other day?'

However, there was indeed a sizeable snake in the middle of the road. I had no idea how dangerous this creature was, and my snake-wrangling skills were not up to much. After a couple of minutes of trying unsuccessfully to get it to move aside, I put a rifle close to its head and fired a blank round, hoping to scare it. Unfortunately, the explosion of the blank cartridge killed it stone dead.

There were a few caustic comments about the pre-briefing and the Major's knowledge of Cypriot wildlife, so I curled up the dead snake and popped it into one of my pouches, in the hope of finding a use for it later.

Instructors always dined together in the Officers Mess and, as the senior officer, Major Gurdon always made a point of arriving last and sitting at the head of the table. That evening, encouraged by my fellow instructors, I placed the dead snake on the Major's chair before his arrival.

He duly marched in, we stood to say grace, and then he pulled back his chair to sit down.

'Oh my God – there's a damn snake on my chair!'

To which all of us replied in glorious unison.

'*There are no snakes in Cyprus!*'

Sadly, the Major did not see the funny side and demanded to know the culprit. I still meet up with him occasionally, but I don't think he has forgiven me to this day.

* * *

The cadets had one free night out during our week in Cyprus, so they all walked down to the local village bars. We instructors decided to escape our charges and drive to Famagusta, which in its heyday had been the major tourist town on the island. There were no tourists any more, but we were told that there was an hotel that regularly put on a racy cabaret show for any British troops permanently based on the island.

As we were preparing to set off in a couple of Army vehicles, the two Army padres wandered by, so we duly invited them both to come along with us. Once we had explained where we were going, Revd Kelly politely declined but, to our delight, Revd Murphy agreed to join us.

'I should probably avoid this night club. But if one is to promote the word of the Lord, then one needs to know the strength of the opposition.'

With a cheer, we all piled into the Land Rovers and set off.

We had dinner and drinks at the hotel and then settled down to watch the cabaret. The hotel manager was Master of Ceremonies and stepped on to the small stage to welcome 'the Officers from the famous Sandhurst Royal Military Academy in England'. He then proceeded, amidst roars and cheers from the audience, to give us the details of the very special show that we were about to see.

However, as we sat in eager anticipation, there was an almighty explosion in the distance and all the lights went out. After a few minutes of confusion, the manager of the hotel announced that a suspected Turkish terrorist had blown up the local electricity sub-station. The power was going to be out for quite some time, so there would be no cabaret show after all.

We all turned to Revd Murphy.

'Did you organize this, padre?!'

His reply was also a classic.

'Not personally, gentlemen – but once you've been *told* what's on the menu, surely you don't need to *see* it all as well, do you?'

* * *

Following my time at Sandhurst, I spent three months at the Army School of Science at Shrivenham, which I best remember for the 'revue' which was put on as a final evening's entertainment at the end of the course.

Taking the mickey out of senior officers was de rigueur in these revues, but it was always a tricky balance to strike between entertaining your colleagues and shooting your career in the foot. I injured my foot on this occasion when I chose to lampoon Shrivenham's Commandant, Major General John Cowtan, giving the Kermit Roosevelt Lecture – an annual exchange of lecturers between the USA and UK military schools that began in 1947 and which continues to this day.

Major General Cowtan was close to retirement at the time. He was an incredible man, a heavily-decorated veteran of the Second World War, having been awarded the Military Cross and Bar. Unfortunately, my irreverence as a young officer with a hankering for the stage knew no boundaries.

Backed up by a colleague playing an ADC to my Major General, I tottered up on to the stage in front of the man himself, surrounded by the whole school, to give my interpretation of his lecture to the great and good of the United States Military Academy at West Point, New York. I don't recall every detail of the script, but here's a snippet that gives enough of a picture of why another senior officer of the British Army had to be added to my growing list of 'Must avoid ...'

Walk up to microphone stand/ Give microphone a tap, at which point it sinks 18 inches in its stand. Try to bend over to speak into it, stumble from side to side until the ADC runs on and re-raises it.

'I'd like to say what a great pleasure it is to be here with you in Canada ...'

Loud stage whisper from ADC: 'No Sir, we're in America, at *West Point*.'

'What Point? Point at what? Are my flies undone ...?'

Fidget inside jacket pockets to find speech notes. Remove various items from pockets including female underwear, grenade, etc. Finally extract speech notes with a flourish.

'Ahem. Take half a pint of milk. Add a chopped onion. Heat over a low stove ... Oh dear, I do apologize. I appear to have my wife's recipe for her dinner tonight. I wonder what her guests will be eating from my speech notes?'

An over-the-top American accent from the audience, played by another colleague ...

'Sir – are you British going to buy the German's Leo-Pard tanks, or our Sheridans?'

'Why, neither, my good fellow – they're obviously both left-hand-drive. No bloody good to us.'

The next day was my last at Shrivenham. On making my farewells I heard what was becoming a familiar phrase from a senior officer who had clearly been present at the previous evening's entertainment.

'Ritchie – you have no future in the Army.'

'No, Sir. Thank you, Sir.'

*   *   *

From its inception in 1802 until 1997, the British Army's Staff College in Camberley, Surrey, was the Army's own College for senior officers, equivalent to the Royal Naval Staff College in Greenwich and the RAF Staff College in Bracknell. On reaching the rank of Major, I spent a year at Camberley along with a motley selection of other newly-promoted or about-to-be promoted young officers.

Some of my fellow students were from foreign military forces, including Major Samir Al Faraq from Egypt. He was a very friendly chap but caught me by surprise one day while we were chatting.

'One thing I must do while I am here in the UK is find the officer who controlled the air strike against Fort Harib in '64. I was there. I'd like to meet the bastard.'

I held out my hand.

'How d'you do?'

We actually became good friends during the rest of our time at the College.

One day, our group was doing a 'TEWT' (Tactical Exercise Without Troops) on Salisbury Plain, on how the Russians might attack us and what action we should take. When I stepped up and gave an analysis of what my team thought might happen, the Commandant got very angry.

'Ritchie! I want to see you alone – come with me.'

When we were out of earshot of the rest of the group, he turned to me red-faced with rage.

'How the hell did your team manage to get hold of the instructors' briefing papers? What you said back there was exactly what is written up!'

'Well, Sir – all I did was ask if any of our foreign students had been to the equivalent Russian Army staff college. It turns out Major Faraq had just been there.'

The instructor who had written up the exercise was called for. Rather red-faced, he admitted that he had asked Major Faraq to provide the instructors' answer to the exercise. That didn't make the Commandant any happier, but he turned on his heel and stormed off.

'What a complete bloody waste of time this has been!'

My unconventional approach, though efficient and accurate, did not win me any extra marks, but I was bought a few drinks that evening.

* * *

My rebellious streak was well exercised when I got the opportunity to be lead scriptwriter of the College's annual pantomime.

We could not decide which of the many classic pantomime stories to base ours on, so I came up with the idea of combining multiple traditional pantomimes into a single, rule-breaking, nose-thumbing extravaganza. And so it was that we staged *Dick Whittington et al*, in which Aladdin, Jack and Cinderella all get arrested by Military Police for appearing in the wrong pantomime, and Prince Charming ends up marrying one of the Ugly Sisters.

Our one and only performance went down very well with the audience, which happened to include Princess Anne and Captain Phillips, although we had to modify our 'Bethlehem Grand Finale' after the Commandant, who was an executive member of CCADD (the Council of Christian Approaches to Defence and Disarmament), attended the dress rehearsal and threw a fit when Joseph emerged from the stable to announce that 'Mary has given birth to a lovely little girl'.

* * *

On leaving Staff College I was posted back to 1st Battalion The Royal Scots, who were in the middle of another four-month tour of Northern Ireland, based at Bessbrook Mill in South Armagh. I was due to take over

Durlston Prep's 1954 production of *The Happiest Days of Your Life*. I'm the one with the earrings.

Wellington College Drill Competition Winners, 1959. I'm front and centre, hogging the camera as usual.

Royal Military Academy Sandhurst, 1961. Robert Parsons in his Morgan with me 'riding shotgun' which was prescient, given the choice of weaponry for my subsequent duel.

Parachute training with 'Les Paras', France, 1961. Mike Nichols, Robert Parsons (6′ 6″) and me. Robert was not permitted to parachute train in Britain as he was too tall for the aircraft doors, but the French were, unsurprisingly, much more laissez-faire.

Forward Air Controller training at RAF Chivenor, 1964, where I got the rare opportunity to take the controls of a Hawker Hunter, which at that time was the world's fastest jet fighter.

The mountainous Radfan region, 1964. Rebels sniping from the mountain tops were a constant threat, but that never crossed my mind while posing for a good picture.

In action as Forward Air Controller with my trusty radio set. 'Send three and fourpence, we're going to a dance.'

The Radfan region. 1964. Water was scarce, but Archie Addison always preferred a bath to a shower. He said it was easier to keep his cigarette lit.

The Radfan region, 1965. Jessie the marauding cow, posing with her conqueror. And no, she was not named after me.

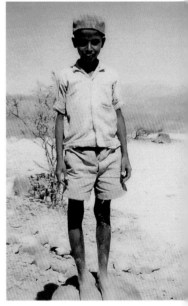

Raga, the young local lad who became my handsomely-paid unofficial batman after I was outsmarted by his (much) older brother.

Napoleon famously rode Marengo the Arab stallion to inspect his troops. I chose Daisy the donkey to entertain my platoon. An army may march on its stomach, but it leans on its funny bone.

adfan, December 1964. Gratefully enjoying a glass of tea with some of the Hujaili tribesmen after e signing of a peace treaty.

From patrolling the rocky terrain of the Jebel Widina in Yemen, to flirting during Government House garden parties in Melbourne, Australia. A difficult transition, but someone had to do it.

Papua New Guinea, 1966. Trying to ingratiate myself with my long-lost aunt and uncle. Fortunately, did not become flavour of the month.

Battalion HQ, Northern Ireland, 1971. A very keen young lad, with mum's permission, helping with some positive PR.

East Germany, 1978, with Sergeant Ray MacDonald of the Royal Scots Dragoon Guards, admiring one of the many helpful signs scattered around East Germany telling us where to look for interesting military sites. One of these signs mysteriously found its way on to my study door back home in Scotland.

A typical overnight location in East Germany while on a trip to photograph 'local flora and fauna'.

Military Mission garden party, Potsdam, 1979. Demonstrating my usual MO of flirting with the military wives, while the men have their backs turned.

A ceremonial handover to my successor in East Germany, Major Willie MacNair. For the photo shoot we hopped into a decommissioned Russian T.55 tank which sat at the entrance to the Soviet Weisswasser training area. Contrary to Western protocol, the keys hadn't been left in the sun visor.

Buckingham Palace, 1981, with mother Iris and brother Alistair, while I proudly show off my MBE awarded 'for stealing'.

Visiting the Royal Marines in Poole, 1981. I couldn't refuse an invitation to take to the water in one of their modified jeeps, but there was no wetsuit small enough to fit me so I went *au naturel*. Kept my Glengarry bonnet on to avoid getting cold.

allykinler, 1981. Some of e fine men and women ˙ the 3rd Battalion, lster Defence Regiment, aciously letting their ommander take centre age.

Northern Ireland, 1981. One of my abiding memories of visiting patrols or roadblocks while commanding 3rd Battalion of the Ulster Defence Regiment was the lack of toilet facilities for a man in his forties. 'Sorry, Sir, you can't go in this field.'

'RSM Johnstone, I'm really struggling here, can you see anything suitable?'

'Would you keep a look out for me, while I ni behind this hedge?'

In 1983 I followed my father into the Queen's Bodyguard for Scotland (Royal Company of Archers). Founded as the Edinburgh Archers in 1676, the Company submitted a request to provide a bodyguard to King George IV for his visit to Scotland in 1822. Its role remains unofficial and is entirely ceremonial.

Our wedding in Greenwich College Chapel, 1984. My darling Araminta has patiently put up with my nonsense ever since, including my usual introduction at social events, 'Have you met my first wife?'

Swaziland, 1986. I am standing next to Major Ginioza, Commander of the Swaziland Royal Warriors, about to be honoured by a 'run past'. If I look apprehensive it's because I was – they are fearsome!

Gambia, 1986. One half of the Ghanaian Navy. The British supplied two naval gunboats and the United States provided the funds to enable us to build the harbour.

Lesotho, 1986. A motherless boy who was being brought up in camp by the men of the Royal Lesotho Defence Force because they did not know which of them was his biological father. Military *esprit de corps* at its best!

Lagos, Nigeria, 1987. General Omu of the Nigerian Army (centre) was a character. We provided his team with a large consignment of 'Blowpipe' surface-to-air missile launchers, which somehow found their way into the hands of the Mujahideen tribesmen in Afghanistan.

ambia, 1987. The Gambian Army proudly demonstrating to me their ingenious Psychological Varfare Unit.

Botswana, 1987. Major General Ian Khama, who had been one of my cadets at Sandhurst from 197 to 1974 and went on to become President of the Republic of Botswana from 2008 to 2018. He is the son of Sir Seretse Khama and Lady Ruth Khama, whose remarkable story was recently made into a excellent film entitled *A United Kingdom*.

Belize, 1987. I shouldn't have tried speaking Belize Creole at the bar to order my pint of snakebite. M companion, for the record, is a non-poisonous tiger tree snake. Doesn't look big enough to eat a tige Or a tree.

Swaziland, 1988. On the range with members of the Ombutfo Swaziland Defence Force.

Belgium, 1992.
Demonstrating UK
defence cuts to the
Italian National
Military Adviser.

Former Yugoslavia,
1993. In my role
as Chief of Staff to
General Jean Cot,
UNPROFOR
Commander,
there were few
opportunities to
make my boss
laugh. But my
French accent was
always a winner.

Paris, 1997. Sir Michael Jay, UK Ambassador to France, with his military attachés, all trying to hold out stomachs in. (L to R) Wing Commander Steve Gunner (Assistant Air Attaché), Air Commodore Peter Eustace (Defence Attaché), HE Sir Michael Jay, self, Captain David Thompson RN (Naval Attaché).

On retiring from the Army in 1997, the doctor advised me to limit myself to one glass of wine a day. I've been diligently following that advice ever since.

command of 'A' Company in Crossmaglen, but again found myself in the position of not being able to take up my new role due to it being mid-tour.

I was therefore given another fill-in role, for a few weeks – in this case, as Planning Officer.

This role mostly involved preparing various daily operational plans, but I was given one major task which was politically extremely sensitive. My job was to plan how to re-draw the border between South Armagh and the Republic of Ireland, based on a 'sensible military tactical boundary'. Of course, it would have been highly controversial had this theoretical idea ever been put into action.

Preparing this plan was not a desk exercise. Together with a wonderful chap called Charlie Hamilton from the RUC, I travelled around the border region in civilian dress, with my military short-back-and-sides grown out, while we photographed and sized up the terrain and made judgements about what alternative border line would give best tactical advantage to the British Army.

Our work took in the town of Newry, which at the time was quite a Republican stronghold. Charlie thought he would give me a taste of the local scene and so, along with a couple of colleagues from RUC Special Branch, he took me to a ceilidh bar in Newry one Sunday evening. I was instructed to keep quiet and let Charlie and his mates buy the drinks – but inevitably, after a few rounds, I insisted it was my turn to stand a round.

Having successfully purchased the drinks, I was making my way back to our table with two glasses in each hand when I collided with a local chap and, in a freakish accident, the hook on his belt snagged the ring on my 9mm pistol which was holstered under my open jacket. My pistol was pulled out and fell to the floor.

Fortunately, the clatter of it falling was lost in the general din of the pub, but the chap whose belt I had snagged looked up from the gun and stared at me for what seemed like an eternity. He then picked up the weapon, stuffed it into the waistband of my trousers, winked at me and with a loud 'Shhh', he moved on, obviously pleased to think that he had quietly helped out a local member of the IRA.

*   *   *

Our HQ at Bessbrook Mill was rather basic. The Mill had been requisitioned by the Army, so we were in a large warehouse which had walled-off rooms without any ceilings. No conversation could be held without everyone in adjoining rooms hearing everything, which gave me the opportunity for a bit of play-acting.

I invented the character of Major Loyalty MacFriland of the non-existent 12th Armagh Battalion of the Ulster Defence Regiment (UDR). At first, I simply practised my 'Norn Iron' accent, which echoed over the temporary walls within our HQ, as Major MacFriland voiced his extremist views on all manner of subjects to entertain my colleagues.

However, for a final flourish at the end of our tour, I somehow convinced my CO to organize a handover meeting between my alter ego and the incoming CO, Lieutenant Colonel Peter Morton of 3 Para, who was visiting for an early recce. For this ridiculous piece of nonsense I got hold of a second-hand UDR uniform from 2nd Battalion and managed to stitch an extra '1' on the jacket's epaulettes to give me my 12th UDR insignia.

My meeting with Lieutenant Colonel Morton was a private one-on-one affair in one of the walled meeting rooms in the Mill – and so it was obviously overheard by all our battalion officers, who were crowded into the adjoining rooms to listen. My Irish accent was convincing enough for the newly arrived officer, who I have to say did a commendable job of humouring my local nutcase while being 'briefed' with useless information.

The meeting ended with my Major MacFriland requesting that, before their departure, 12th Battalion be permitted to hold their Annual Camp on the Gaelic Sports field in Crossmaglen, along with beating a Retreat with our pipes and drums in the main town square. The bemused Colonel Morton replied with a thoroughly professional 'I think not!'

*   *   *

Our next tour took us back to Germany, where we took over as the Nuclear Convoy Escort Battalion. This was obviously a pretty important task for the 1st Battalion; we went on regular exercises with a convoy of mobile launch vehicles carrying live nuclear warheads. My other significant and much more demanding responsibility was as President of the Officers' Mess Committee.

Many of the parties we held at the Mess had a mixture of German and British guests. An early lesson for me as President was to have invitations to German guests always indicate a 7.00pm start, and those to British guests indicate a 6.30pm start – as a result, everyone arrived together promptly at 7.00pm.

As well as the Officers' Mess and the Sergeants' Mess, all the teachers from the Army's primary and secondary schools lived in their own equivalent accommodation – called, with an astonishing leap of imagination, the Teachers' Mess. Parties at the Teachers' Mess were always great fun, as the teachers, who worked very hard, needed to let their hair down occasionally just like the rest of us.

One such event was a 'Bad Taste Party', at which there was a prize for whoever could dress to cause the greatest offence. I went as a failed kamikaze pilot who, on approaching a Royal Navy aircraft carrier, had lost his nerve and chosen to make a perfect landing on it instead. Captain James Mainwaring Burton of the Welsh Guards arrived wrapped head to foot in bandages, with three bottles of tomato ketchup splashed over his torso, and proudly announced he was a used sanitary towel.

There were various other very offensive characters – but none quite like Mike Cran. Mike's entrance to the party begun with the arrival of an Army truck which drove on to the lawn outside the Teachers' Mess. Two chaps jumped out and proceeded to dig a post hole in the middle of the lawn. They then returned to the truck and emerged with Mike, tied to a massive wooden cross and wearing nothing but a loin cloth. He was duly placed upright in the fresh post-hole in the lawn.

This caused quite some uproar, not least with the school's headmaster, a rather religious man who started yelling for Mike to be removed at once.

'Take that obscenity off my lawn immediately!'

'Certainly, Headmaster. Can we first just confirm that this is the prize-winner?'

'Yes, yes, no question – just get rid of him!'

And so Jesus was duly removed from the cross by a kamikaze pilot, a vampire, and a bearded nun in basque and stockings. Having made a name for himself as a used sanitary towel, Captain James Mainwaring Burton went on to become Equerry to Her Majesty the Queen Mother.

* * *

Part of the role of a senior officer is to administer an appropriate punishment when a soldier steps out of line.

Corporal Gallacher was brought before me one morning. He had been the Duty NCO at the 'A' Company Bar the previous evening and, instead of getting the takings locked up in the guardroom for the night before they were deposited the next morning with the paymaster, he had blown the lot on treating himself and a few mates to a very expensive late night at a local bar in town.

I ordered him to be put under close arrest in the guardroom for 48 hours, in the hope that this would make him see the error of his ways, especially as I knew he had recently married a local German girl and so would then have her wrath to deal with as well.

What I *didn't* know, however, was that the couple had a very young baby. I discovered this a few hours after the Lance Corporal had been locked up, when his wife appeared in my office with the baby and proceeded to harangue me in broken English about how she needed her husband to look after the youngster while she went to work.

She called me everything under the sun, and with a final Germanic curse claimed that I now had to look after the baby. She then put the little critter down on my desk (in my in-tray, no less) and stormed out.

The baby lay there looking up at me innocently, while I sat at my desk pondering what to do. In any strange or unusual situation, the Company Clerk tends to be the first port of call.

'Corporal Atkinson – can you step into my office, please?'

I lifted the baby up from my in-tray and placed it in my out-tray. Then, as the Corporal came in, I gave him a very common order, one that he had received many times in the past.

'Corporal – clear my out-tray, please.'

'Yes, Sir, right away.'

Without missing a beat, the good Corporal picked up the baby, tucked it under his arm, grabbed the few papers that constituted my work effort for the morning and marched out with the lot.

I discovered afterwards that Corporal Atkinson duly turned for assistance to the Company Sergeant Major, who recognized the baby and put two and two together. In the end, the Sergeant Major's wife stepped into the breach and looked after the baby until its mother returned.

As for Gallacher himself – well, if the tongue-lashing that I had received from his wife was any guide, I imagine he had a rather chastening experience on his eventual return home.

* * *

We had as part of our Officers' Mess a beautiful old building which had previously served as an Officers' Mess for the German Army. It was said to be haunted – but then, that can be said of most old buildings. Downstairs there was a wonderful large ballroom, ideal for Scottish country dancing. There were only four suites of rooms upstairs, but they were charming and luxurious, so I was delighted to be accommodated there along with a few other lucky officers.

One night, I was woken around midnight by an almighty din from the ballroom. Chairs were being dragged across the room, there were shouts and yells and general chaos. Clearly a party was in full swing, presumably led by our young lieutenants. I was furious – not only were they disturbing my beauty sleep, but I hadn't been invited to the party.

I stomped grumpily out onto the landing , where I was met by Captain David Dickson who had been similarly rudely awakened.

'What the devil is going on downstairs?'

'I don't know, but they are about to get a piece of my mind!'

'Likewise!'

We marched down the staircase and across the hall in shared indignation, but as we were yards from the door to the ballroom, the noise suddenly stopped. Completely.

We paused and looked at each other for no more than a second or two, then flung open the doors to find – a completely empty ballroom. No revellers, no furniture, no chaos. Nothing but silence.

It would have been impossible to clear the room in the few seconds that it had taken David and me to reach the doorway. However, not wanting to believe in the old ghost stories, the next day, I carried out a thorough interview process of all the other officers. But every one of them was insistent that they had been nowhere near the Mess Ballroom the previous evening.

* * *

We regularly held 'Sunday Curry Lunches' at the Mess. Officers and their wives and guests, including children, would enjoy a relaxing lunch together, with a few drinks for the grown-ups and games for the children.

A local chap by the name of Hamon Peresse was a guest one Sunday with his wife and young son. Most children were very well behaved in such an environment, but Hamon's son Yann was a bit of a handful. We caught the youngster more than once swigging from glasses when the adults weren't looking. But Hamon was a charming chap, and so we were happy to indulge him and his boisterous lad.

Unfortunately, Hamon enjoyed himself a little too much as well – so much so that he was stopped by the local police while driving home. The police were armed with a new type of breathalyser, which they were keen to try out. Hamon knew he was in trouble and, indeed, once he had been shown how to use the machine, it duly indicated that he was well over the legal limit. Hamon began to plead for leniency, but his son Yann was making a terrible fuss in the back seat, wanting to 'blow the balloon, blow the balloon' too, and so Hamon made a plea to the police officer.

'I know I'm in trouble, officer, but to keep my son quiet while you deal with me, could you possibly let him blow into the breathalyser?'

The police officer must have been having a good day, since he happily put on a fresh mouthpiece, reset the breathalyser and held it while the young lad puffed away. Imagine his surprise when the indicator showed that a six-year-old was also well over the drink-drive limit.

Of course, Hamon was not aware of what his son had been up to at the party and so took this result as a gift from above.

'Oh dear, officer – it looks like your new system must be faulty!'

'Hmmm. Yes, sir, I believe it must be. I suppose you'd better be on your way ...'

It was only when Hamon next attended one of our lunches and told us of his story of the lucky escape that we were able to put him straight about the facts of the matter.

* * *

After a few days leave back in the UK, I was driving to Hull to catch the ferry to Rotterdam. I owned a rather clapped-out Toyota at the time, which struggled to get above 50mph. A further complication involved a traffic accident on the A1 which held me up. As a result, I was running late.

I therefore have to confess that I started to push my luck as I got closer to my destination. I was doing over 40mph through the outskirts of Hull when I was duly pulled over by the local traffic police for speeding in a 30mph zone. I apologized to the officer and explained that there had been an accident on the A1 which had held me up – not that it was a valid excuse, of course.

I then showed my ID and explained that I was Major Charles Ritchie of The Royal Scots and I was due in Munster the next morning.

'No need to be speeding, though, Major.'

'I do appreciate that, officer – but I've simply got to catch my ferry.'

'Oh, really, Major? And why is that?'

'Well, I have an urgent operational exercise that I simply must attend tomorrow morning.'

'Urgent, eh? And what would that be?'

'Well, you see, I'm commanding a military escort.'

'Military escort, eh? Someone important, then?'

'Er, well … no not someone … some*thing*.'

I felt the police officer was tiring of the game, so I had to go all-in.

'Officer, if you must know … I'm going to be escorting the movement of live nuclear weapons across Germany. I know I'm guilty of speeding, so if you could, will you please book me and let me get on my way, or I will definitely miss my ferry.'

The officer raised a bushy but enigmatic eyebrow.

'Hmm. Just a minute, Major.'

As I hopped from one foot to the other in agitation, the officer got on his radio and had a brief conversation with, presumably, his superior. He then turned back to me with a very serious demeanour.

'Right, Major – I've to give you the mother of all rollockings, and then get you to the ferry terminal. We'll radio ahead to hold the ferry's departure – follow us.'

And with that, I was led through the outskirts of Hull by the patrol car with full sirens blaring and lights flashing, right up to the ramp at the ferry itself, which indeed had been held back a few minutes for my arrival. With a cheery wave to the nice police officer, who had done his bit to secure the safety of the Western world for another day, I was on my way.

As a postscript, I subsequently wrote a letter to the Chief Constable, on my official Nuclear Convoy Escort Battalion headed notepaper, quoting his officer's name and thanking him and his superior officer for their understanding and assistance. Just so that policeman knew for certain that he hadn't been hoodwinked.

Chapter 9

Exit, Pursued by a Russian Bear

My next posting, in the rank of Major, was as Operations Officer for the British Commanders-in-Chief Mission (BRIXMIS) to the Headquarters of the Group of Soviet Forces in Germany. I was there from March 1978 to October 1980.

BRIXMIS was one of the three Military Liaison Missions that had been formed at the end of the Second World War, originally designed to keep communications open between each of the Western Allies (UK, USA and France) and the Soviets. There were thirty-one Russians with freedom of movement in the British Zone of West Germany, and in exchange we had thirty-one Britons based in East Germany – twenty Army and eleven RAF. The Americans and French each had a similar arrangement, although with fewer personnel as their Zones were smaller.

The Soviets provided us with accommodation in Potsdam in East Germany, and we did the same for their Mission in West Germany. However, living conditions in Potsdam were so difficult, with daily queues for fresh food and the like, that we all lived in West Berlin and used the Military Mission House provided for us in Potsdam purely as a daytime base.

* * *

I was formally described as a Liaison Officer, and my official role was to look at movement between West Germany and West Berlin, assist with the management of war graves, organize and attend various ceremonies and arrange liaison visits between the Russians and the British. But my real job, involving the other thirty British military personnel assigned to BRIXMIS, was to organize the constant operation of intelligence-gathering on the 6,500-plus Soviet and East German barracks, training areas, radar sites and missile sites, and all their related military movements.

I was one of only two British members in BRIXMIS who didn't speak Russian. This put me at a disadvantage, but I had been selected for my knowledge of German and French. I would meet every week with my French and American counterparts to agree which of our teams would recce each region of East Germany.

As with all BRIXMIS members, I was issued with a Soviet Army ID card. Each morning, I would travel from West Berlin to Potsdam, exchanging my British Army ID card for a Soviet Army ID card at the checkpoint on the Glienicke Bridge, now much better known as the 'Bridge of Spies' – very aptly as far as I am concerned, since my role and that of my fellow Mission officers was fundamentally one of covert espionage. The Russians and East Germans knew what we were doing and, equally, we knew that their Mission members in West Germany were doing the same. The game was to not get caught in the act. We did not go as far as to break into buildings or cause any wilful damage, though we would steal anything we thought we could get away with, particularly documents.

The handover from my predecessor, Major Ted Taylor, took a full six months, as he took me on tours to show me as many as thirty different sites each day that could be of potential interest. The Russians had helpfully put up lots of 'Military Mission' signs, each warning that the passage of any Military Liaison Mission personnel was forbidden beyond that point – which simply confirmed for us where the military sites of interest were located! Needless to say, these signs often disappeared when we were in the area, so that we could plead ignorance if we were caught getting too close for comfort. A quick recce to check no-one was watching, chuck the sign in the boot of our large car, then sell it as a memento or curio back in West Berlin. I still have one in my study.

*   *   *

As Liaison officers we would also do cultural 'town tours', which involved an official Mission visit to a particular town or city where, along with a Tour NCO and an official driver, we visited art galleries and theatres, did some shopping and enjoyed the local night life. These town tours were deliberately intended to show us carrying out a tourist visit and behaving normally, in service dress uniforms rather than patrol dress of jersey, trousers and boots.

In contrast with town tours, our patrol tours lasted two or three days and were a cover for intelligence-gathering activities, during which we would try to visit as many points of military interest as possible. Our vehicles were specially adapted for such operations – infra-red headlights, heavy armour-plating, four-wheel drive, etc. The standard approach was that I would sit in the back of the car map-reading and taking photographs, with the accompanying Tour NCO, a trained expert, identifying every piece of Soviet military equipment we came across.

* * *

I had an early introduction to the dangers of my new role while on my first ever tour with Major Taylor in East Germany, as part of his handover to me.

We were driving through Treuenbrietzen, a town south of Potsdam, in our official Military Mission car and had stopped at a level crossing while a train rolled by. As we waited for the barriers to be raised, a massive Russian MAZ-543 eight-wheeled SCUD-B surface-to-surface missile launcher approached from the opposite side of the track. As the train departed, we could see the Russian officer in the cab of this monster vehicle pointing out our car to his driver. As soon as the barriers rose, the huge beast pulled across the road towards us.

Before our driver could react, the massive vehicle's offside wheels started to roll up the bonnet of our car. I genuinely thought that my time had come. So much for a Cold War nuclear holocaust ending the world, I was about to be killed by a nuclear missile being slowly driven over me.

We all flung ourselves into the footwells of the car while the deafening noise of glass shattering, metal bending and tyres exploding told us that we were getting properly harassed. Thankfully, the reinforced steel shell of our armour-plated Opel Admiral held out, and we managed to crawl out relatively unscathed from a window of the mangled car.

The Russians were milling about but refused to help us. Fortunately, a passing East German taxi driver agreed to take me to his house to make a phone call to the Mission in Potsdam, which promptly sent out a recovery vehicle. We were taken back to West Germany along with the wrecked car, and there followed a most intense diplomatic exchange, the only result of which was that we had a formal apology from the Russians for the 'unfortunate error of a brand-new trainee driver, who will be disciplined appropriately'.

We arranged for a hamper of excellent food and drink to be dropped off discreetly at the back door of the friendly taxi driver at 3.00am one night, as a thank you for the risk he had taken in helping us.

* * *

Another scare tactic which our hosts employed was to arrest us and keep us locked in a cell for a few hours. I was once arrested on a trumped-up charge while on a routine tour and taken to a nearby Soviet Army barracks, where I was put in a cell cage next to a variety of young Russian soldiers in individual cages who presumably had committed various misdemeanours.

My training for BRIXMIS had included a three-day course with the SAS on surviving capture and interrogation, in which I was given the task of breaking into a military base somewhere in the South of England, photographing a particular piece of military equipment, and then getting out undetected. Needless to say, I was captured in the act and then put through an extreme form of interrogation, including being kept naked in an empty cell for 24 hours without food, and regularly sprayed with cold water to stop me sleeping – even put through a form of waterboarding, which was extremely unpleasant. They also threatened me with a cavity search. I didn't know they allowed dentists in the SAS.

Compared to my training experience, my time in the Soviet Army cell was straightforward, apart from one aspect. I had only been locked up for a short time, when the young soldier in the next cage to me was taken out of his cell, yelling and screaming. He was led to the courtyard outside where I could see through the main door that they were tying him to a post. The main door was then closed, removing the poor chap from view, a command was barked out and a volley of shots was fired, followed by silence.

One of the guards then came back in to clear the youngster's cell. He took one look at me, pointed and grinned.

'You – next!'

For the next few hours I followed my regimental motto of 'Panic With Dignity', before I was released with an apology about 'a misunderstanding'.

I don't know to this day whether the firing squad was simply an act put on for my benefit, or a real execution. Either way, it had the desired effect of scaring me witless.

*   *   *

Despite living in West Berlin, we still had to suffer the awful daily meals supplied by the Russians to our Mission House. Our American cousins were suffering a similar plight, until they came up with an ingenious plan. One day, when the Russian meal delivery arrived at their Mission House in Potsdam, they immediately loaded it into a refrigerated truck, drove it across the Glienicke Bridge to the USA airfield in West Berlin and put it on a military flight. It was then flown straight to West Germany, where it was promptly delivered to the Russian Military Mission as their daily meal, in place of the usual top-quality American fare.

On experiencing this sudden drop in culinary quality, the head of the Russian Military Mission went berserk, ordered a sample of the delivered food to be put in a car, and was driven to see the Chief of Staff in the American Military HQ. He then proceeded to go off on a major rant about how appalled he was at the disgraceful quality of the meal that had just been delivered to his Mission members that day.

The American General had been well briefed in advance and patiently bided his time. When his Russian guest had exhausted his ranting, he quietly and calmly explained that the delivered food that had caused such distress was the very same that had been supplied by Russian colleagues to the American Mission in Potsdam a few hours earlier.

From that day on, the meals delivered to the American, British and French Mission Houses in Potsdam were always first class.

*   *   *

We used to throw regular parties at our Mission House for key Russian guests as well as a few from the French and American Missions. We always served great food, champagne and all other manner of drinks, although it was amusing to see that the Russians loved our gins and tonic more than anything else, as they could not get hold of this for themselves.

Before the first party following my arrival, I was given a detailed briefing on how to act as host, including how our Russian guests were welcomed, shown around and entertained. It was important that I made sure I introduced myself to every member of the Soviet External Relations Branch ('SERB') that BRIXMIS dealt with on a day-to-day basis, as well as any senior Russian Army officers who had been invited. This could include the likes of the Commander-in-Chief of the Soviet Army in East Germany, Colonel General Grinkevitch, depending on which senior guests we had attending from our side.

I also learned that our Mission had developed a particular approach in dealing with the Russian wives. Specifically, all the Russian wives congregated in the main entrance hallway while their husbands went on ahead into the party. When the most senior Russian officer's wife arrived, she would disappear into the ladies' loo with a large empty bag, only to come out a few minutes later with clearly quite a lot in her now-bulging bag. The wife of the next most senior officer then went in, similarly carrying an empty bag that was then bulging on exit. This process continued until all the wives had paid their visit to the ladies.

I was bemused by this behaviour, until it was explained to me how difficult it was for Russian women to get hold of quality toiletries such as perfume, shampoo, moisturising lotion and the like. So our staff would fill the ladies' loo with a broad range of toiletries brought over from West Germany that were unavailable in the East, and the Russian wives would take it in turn to help themselves to a selection. Then, with their wives happy, the Russian officers would relax and enjoy themselves, meaning we could ingratiate ourselves a little further. The unspoken agreement was that the rest of the evening could go ahead without fear of anything else being 'half-inched'.

* * *

Our parties, as well as those held by our American and French allies, were useful in keeping relations amicable, but they rarely gave me any opportunity for intelligence-gathering, due to my inability to speak Russian. Most of the Soviets did speak some English, but they would often try to catch me out by saying something to me in Russian. When I responded with one of my few stock phrases – 'I'm sorry, I don't understand' – they would smile and wink enigmatically, tap their nose discreetly and say, 'Of course, Major, I forgot you don't speak Russian ...' Cheeky blighters never did believe me.

On the rare occasions when we were invited to a party in the Russian Mission, I would prepare myself with the old MI6 trick of eating two bread rolls slathered thickly with lard and washed down with a pint of milk, which lined the stomach so completely that very little alcohol would get digested. I could then accept all the hospitality that could be poured at me, keep my wits about me without giving away any state secrets and, at the end of the evening, walk away from the table while our hosts gradually slipped under it, muttering curses about 'how can that mad Scotsman hold his drink?'

* * *

The East German currency, the Ostmark (Eastern mark), was officially kept at parity with the West German Deutschmark. However, due to the limited usefulness of the former outside of East Germany, there was an active black market in which one could obtain five Ostmarks for every Deutschmark. There were rules to force visitors to East German to exchange a certain amount of currency on entry, but military personnel were excluded from this. As a result, any spending we did in East Germany was normally in currency obtained at a very favourable 5:1 exchange rate on the black market – very naughty.

That said, there was not terribly much in East Germany to spend your money on. However, one exception was the wonderful operatic performances that were regularly held in East Berlin. As a bachelor, one of the ways that I used to repay the hospitality of friends or acquaintances was to take guests from West Berlin across Checkpoint Charlie into East Berlin, to have dinner at one of the best restaurants and take in an opera. The operas in East Berlin were typically of excellent quality, and they were all subsidised. I could treat a party of four to the best seats in the house, champagne at the interval and a top-quality dinner afterwards with drinks, for the total equivalent of ten pounds sterling for all four of us.

At a more basic level, a decent bottle of vodka was so cheap that we used it in our cars' windscreen washers, as it was cheaper than washer fluid and it didn't freeze as easily. This was also a benefit when out on overnight tours during the winter – we couldn't possibly take any glass bottles of alcohol with us on our tours, or even hipflasks, but it wasn't unusual to take a quick squirt from the windscreen washer into a mug, before climbing into our sleeping bags.

* * *

Although the Russian military resented our presence, they very rarely followed us as we went about our business. It was very much tit-for-tat – if they gave us a hard time, the same would happen to their guys in West Germany.

The biggest problem for all three Allied military missions was the Stasi, the East German Ministry for State Security. The Stasi applied a lot of manpower to monitoring and, on many occasions, deliberately getting in our way as we discreetly tried to perform our intelligence-gathering roles.

The Stasi tailed us most days as we drove around the country and made no attempt to be discreet. We knew that they were following us, and they knew that we knew, but that was all part of the game. On regular occasions, to break the monotony, they would block in our car so that we couldn't move, while they called in their Russian counterparts to accuse us of some random misdemeanour or other.

As well as my early encounter with the missile transporter, I was also nearly rammed by a Russian truck as we were driving away from a train station where we had been monitoring some passing military equipment on rail flatbeds. Our driver managed to evade the oncoming truck, but only by swerving into a wooden fence and driving across two or three gardens, before managing to get back on the road and make our escape.

One of the French Mission's warrant officers was not so lucky. His car was deliberately struck side-on by a Russian truck, and he was killed outright. There was obviously a hell of a stink about that, although the Russians trotted out their usual excuse about 'an accident involving a learner driver'.

* * *

We were on a routine tour on the banks of the River Elbe, checking to see if there was any military activity. The Russians would occasionally use this particular area to do river-crossing exercises and the like, and we had heard that there was something currently being prepared.

As we drove along the grass bank by the riverside, we noticed a young boy on a bicycle waving frantically at us. Our driver was about to drive past the boy when he picked up his bicycle and threw it in front of the car! Well, that certainly stopped us – but not before we flattened the bike, which caused the young chap to burst into tears.

I got out of the car and in my best German asked the boy what he was playing at. Through his sobbing, he tried to explain.

'I like the British Mission [sniff]. You … you sometimes give me chocolate, and … and … chewing gum [sniff]. So … I … I didn't want you to fall into the hole.'

We had no idea what he meant, but he then led us fifty yards further along the riverbank, where we were amazed to find that the Russians had dug a car-trap for us. It was a huge pit about ten feet deep, overlaid with thin wooden planks lightly covered with turf. Clearly, their aim was that we would drive into it, which is exactly what would have happened had our young friend not stopped us by sacrificing his bicycle.

We obviously had to make reparations for the bike. I arranged to meet the boy's father the following Saturday night. Having made sure we had not been followed, I handed over a brand new bicycle, paid for by a withdrawal of cash from our Mission slush fund. The father thanked me profusely, and it was nice to see the youngster proudly pedalling up and down the village streets a few days later on his gleaming new bicycle.

* * *

My favourite escapade with the Stasi was on a routine tour when, as usual, we were being followed by a couple of Stasi officers. We were having rather a boring day, so we decided to stop and have a picnic lunch in a field by a canal. We parked our car in the field. and the Stasi dutifully parked a hundred yards away.

There were three of us – driver, tour NCO and me – and only two of them. So I suggested to my colleagues that we should have a bit of fun with these young Stasi.

After we had eaten our lunch, I wandered away towards a wood at the edge of the field about a quarter of a mile away. As expected, one of the Stasi officers got out of their car and followed me. Ten minutes later, as we had agreed, my NCO got up and headed after me. As expected, the second Stasi followed him. When we met at the edge of the wood, our driver then rapidly drove our car across the field up to us, we jumped in and sped back to the canal, where the Stasi had left their car – hotly pursued by the two of them, running back as fast as their legs could carry them.

The keys were still in their car, which was a schoolboy error, so I promptly locked it and, turning to give our Stasi friends a cheery wave as they angrily galloped towards us, tossed the keys into the canal. Then we roared off, chortling.

Looking back on it, we were simply having rather a boring day, so I thought we could teach the Stasi a lesson. However, it was quite a childish prank and it backfired on me. From then on, wherever I went, I often had two and sometimes even three cars following and harassing me, usually by blocking our car from moving.

I therefore had to develop my own strategies to combat this. One tactic when being followed by the Stasi was to take our four-wheel-drive car into a muddy field. The Stasi car would dutifully follow us and usually get stuck, allowing us to make a muddy getaway, waving politely to them as we departed.

Once when pulling this trick, I recognized the two Stasi officers in the car behind as 'regulars' who frequently chose to spend their day following us and whom we had evaded via the muddy-field trick not more than a week ago. Having succeeded in getting them stuck for a second time, we stopped and approached them for a chat. After some hesitation on their part, a deal was struck – we would pull them out and save them the embarrassment of reporting this repeated disaster to their bosses, if they would stop following us in the future.

It worked – we never saw that pair again.

But my favourite, being such a showman by nature, was the 'loco vocal local' tactic. This was deployed whenever our car was deliberately blocked in the street, and it involved entertaining passers-by and shaming the Stasi by yelling GDR slogans in my best German.

'*Ich lebe hier in das Paradies der Arbeiterklasse!*' ['I am living here in the paradise of the working class!']

'*Ich bin Tiel von das Paradies!*' ['I am part of the Paradise!']

That would usually get a laughing crowd gathering around, while the Stasi who had blocked me in became ever more agitated. They would tell me to shut up, but the crowd would cry for an encore, so I would put on my Glengarry or my Tam O'Shanter and go for broke.

'*Ich bin Major in der Befreiungsarmee der Schottischen Volke!*' ['I am a Major in the Scottish People's Liberation Army!']

If I succeeded in creating enough of a scene, the Stasi would crumble with embarrassment, move their cars and tell us to clear off. No doubt about it – laughter is the best weapon.

* * *

Early one evening, having set off on quite an important surveillance task, we noticed that we were being followed by a car with a West German licence plate. That was unusual. Two young men were in the car, but I assumed they were civilians visiting family in East Germany or something like that, and who were simply taking a curious interest in us.

It was our driver who first became suspicious.

'Excuse me, Sir, but there is something very odd about that car. They are keeping a standard distance from us.'

He slowed down, and so did they. He let cars overtake us, and so did they. This was classic Stasi behaviour, but we knew most of the cars that the Stasi used. A smart BMW with a West German licence plate was not their style.

Rather than stand down from the task and just lead these strangers on a wild goose chase to frustrate them, I was keen for us to try to shake them off. The first thing we tried was to go the wrong way down a one-way street. The young men simply followed us. We tried the same again, but this time we stopped by the no-entry sign and I opened my window and pointed up at it. Again, they simply followed us in our illegal manoeuvre.

I then pointed my camera at them through the back window. No Stasi would ever want to have his picture distributed among the Allied intelligence communities. They did their best to hide their faces, but they did not draw back from tailing us.

By this stage I was pretty sure that they were indeed Stasi, so we had to up the ante. Darkness had fallen, which we could use to our advantage.

Our driver on that night was up for the challenge. He had presumably been a getaway driver for an East End mob before enlisting, because he executed my instructions perfectly. We drove slowly out of town and, checking my map, I could see we were on a road that eventually came to a T-junction. I used the map to calculate the exact distance to the junction and reset the car's tripometer to zero. Our driver then floored the accelerator.

As we raced along the road at over 100mph, with our pursuers hot on our heels, I watched the tripometer and kept calling out the remaining distance to the T-junction. With 100m to go, we switched off our tail-lights and brake lights, the driver braked hard, spun the car to the left, floored the accelerator again, counter-steered against the sliding tyres and just managed to stay on the tarmac. As we fish-tailed away down the road, I turned back to watch.

The chasing driver obviously did not know the road layout. Without seeing any brake lights ahead of him as a warning, he drove his car at some speed straight across the T-junction, where it then completely disappeared from view.

I yelled for us to stop and we ran back to the junction, hoping to find the car simply stuck in a ditch, with two grumpy and possibly bruised Stasi officers inside. But there was simply no sign of the car whatsoever. We found a track on the side of the road leading sharply downhill, which we followed with increasing concern until we came to the edge of a quarry, at the bottom of which we could see the car, totally wrecked. It was obvious that the two passengers were dead, but we checked to make sure. There was also plenty of evidence – radio equipment, assault rifles, pistols, flares and so on – that our pursuers were indeed Stasi officers.

I felt awful for the poor unfortunate young men. But there was nothing we could do for them now – and we had to make ourselves scarce before their support arrived. We drove for several hours to put as much distance as possible between us and the scene of the accident. We ended up at a disused barn we knew of, where we cooked a meal, making sure to leave lots of evidence of it, and caught a couple of hours sleep. The next morning, I headed into a nearby village, as we were aware that the local shopkeeper was a keen informant for the Stasi. I made a point of chatting to him, spinning a yarn about how we had spent a lovely evening camping by the barn, cooked a meal, had a great full night's sleep, etc … all to try to manufacture an alibi, knowing that he would be sure to visit the barn when we left, to check us out.

On our return to West Berlin, we discovered that the BMW had been seized by the Stasi a few weeks earlier following a failed attempt to smuggle people across the border to West Germany, and they had simply requisitioned the vehicle for their own use.

We heard nothing more about the incident for the remainder of my time in East Germany. No action was taken by the East Germans, despite knowing that I had been the target that the unfortunate Stasi officers had been ordered to follow. One factor that may have played a part is that I was a BRIXMIS officer with a Soviet ID card. It could have created quite a complicated political affair for an officer of the Soviet Army to be accused by the East Germans.

It was only when I had returned to the UK that it was confirmed that I had indeed been blamed by the East Germans for the death of the two Stasi officers. MI6 informed me that I was not to return there under any circumstances for at least 25 years – effectively the statute of limitations under German law.

* * *

Given all my run-ins with the Stasi, it was fascinating to obtain, only quite recently, the file which they had built up on me all those years ago. In fact, since 2018, anybody who has ever served in the British Military Mission has been able to obtain a full copy of their personal Stasi file.

In my case, for example, it confirmed what we had suspected all along. All the staff in the Mission House in Potsdam, from the cook to the gardeners to the chambermaids, were members of the Stasi. I must say I was slightly disappointed to have it confirmed, by reading my file, that the pretty chambermaid in the Mission House, who I thought was 'sweet' on me, was actually simply acting on orders to try to seduce me, for blackmailing purposes.

We had all been warned of such tactics at the time and, for the most part, everyone avoided such honey-traps. However, one member of the British Mission did, unfortunately, succumb. He was a charming, handsome character – married with children, but always one for chatting up the ladies.

He had been with us a while when I sent him on his first 'town tour'. I gave him his briefing: walk around, do some shopping, visit a restaurant, attend a concert if there is one, go to the hotel bar. Basically, act as a law-abiding tourist – but behave yourself!

The following Sunday afternoon, I was in my flat in West Berlin when I received a phone call from him, sounding very distressed. I told him to come straight over, and when he arrived he was practically in tears.

'Charles – I've been very, very stupid. I was in the bar last night with my driver … I got talking to a very nice young girl who told me she had missed her last bus home and she did not have enough money for a taxi. She asked if she could sleep in my room for the night … and she was so nice to me … so … so I said yes.'

'You idiot!'

'I know, Charles, but I thought it would be okay. But when we got in to the room, she got undressed … and I got undressed … and we got into bed together … and then I heard the door open and two gorillas burst in and starting taking photos. The girl was screaming and pulling the sheets off me, and … I'm afraid … well … I think they managed to get *very* embarrassing photos of me naked.'

'OK, we need to tell the boss immediately.'

I rang the Brigadier, who asked us to go straight round to see him. Once the distraught fellow had told his story once more, the Brigadier sighed and turned to me.

'Charles – you know the drill – get on with it. Brief me in the morning.'

We knew what had to be done in these circumstances. The chap had been set up and primed for blackmail and so we had to defuse the situation. I explained to him that he had to go home immediately, tell his wife everything that had happened and ask for her forgiveness. If she was willing to forgive him, then she had to phone me herself and tell me.

About two hours later, I got a call from his wife. Choking back her tears, she told me that her husband had explained everything and that she did indeed forgive him for what had happened.

The attempted blackmail then played out as we expected, and our beleaguered target carried out my instructions to the letter. At the next party held by the Russians, in Potsdam, a Russian officer sidled up to him, suggested that they needed a 'man-to-man conversation', then led him away to a side room. Our man returned a few minutes later and gave me a little nod to say that things had gone to plan, although it wasn't until the debrief the next day that we got the full story.

As predicted, he had been taken to a room where, laid out on a table, there was a display of photographs of him with the girl. He was indeed naked as the day he was born, yet proudly standing to attention, as it were.

As per the script, our man sat down in front of the incriminating evidence and stared at it intently, while his Russian guest presented his proposed 'solution'.

'Obviously we would hate for your wife and everyone else to see these pictures. So, out of friendship and respect, we will destroy all these pictures, including the negatives, if you simply let us have one very small thing – the British Military telephone directory for West Berlin.'

In terms of secret information, our telephone directory was hardly going to win the Cold War for the Russians. However, it was an officially restricted document and, while its contents were immaterial, if you handed it over then the Russians could use the fact that you had given them one restricted document to coerce you into providing another, and another, and so on – increasing the classification value each time.

After a long pause, our chap stood up.

'I can't possibly give you any military documents. But ...'

The Russian officer leaned in eagerly to hear the counter-offer.

'... could I please have copies of these two particular photos here ... oh, and this one ... and an enlargement of this excellent one?'

The Russian muttered a curse, realizing he was not going to get anywhere. Any leverage had clearly already been undermined by our side and dealt with. He quietly folded up all the photographs, made a point of tearing them up and threw them in the waste-paper basket.

'Okay, my friend – this time, count yourself lucky.'

* * *

My parents decided at short notice that they would come out to visit me in West Berlin. I must have owed them money or something.

I quickly put together a plan of how to keep them occupied and out of trouble during their visit, with trips to the opera, sightseeing and the like.

It so happened that their visit coincided with the annual Allied Forces Day Parade, where the British, American and French military all paraded through West Berlin – a stirring sight to see and therefore a 'must' for my parents' visit. Much more importantly, I wanted to get them tickets to the evening reception hosted by the Mayor of Berlin, where they could rub shoulders with the great and the good, and even their son as well.

I put a phone call in to Alex Crichton, who was the ADC to General Bob Richardson, Commandant of the British Sector in Berlin. Alex was organizing the British element of the parade and associated events. I explained my need to get tickets to the reception, but Alex was not forthcoming.

'Sorry, Charles – everyone wants to go, all the tickets are taken, there's a waiting list.'

'But Alex ...'

'No, I can't possibly allow your parents to jump the queue, as they are only visitors and all that. Nothing I can do – sorry.'

General Richardson was from The Royal Scots and in my past postings, on the odd stage revue and such, I had learned to do a passable impersonation of him. If Alex wouldn't budge for Major Charles Ritchie, maybe he would for the General himself.

I prepared my lines and, the next morning, I telephoned down to Alex again, using my best Bob Richardson voice – which I would loosely describe as a combination of Prince Philip and Sean Connery, with a dollop of Laurence Olivier and perhaps a dash of Churchill for good measure.

'Ah ... .hello, Alexsh.'

To my delight, Alex immediately took the bait.

'Oh, hello, Sir!'

'Now, er, shee here Alexsh ... . I'd, er, like to have shum words about the official guesht list for the Mayor'sh resheption ... there jusht might be shum people I'd like to invite.'

'No problem, Sir – I'll bring the guest list to you right away.'

Before I could stop him, Alex had put the phone down, presumably to nip along to the General's office in person with the guest list. Oh blast, how efficient of him – I hadn't planned for this!

I leapt out of my chair and ran out of my office, which was on the top floor, and clattered down several flights of stairs, three steps at a time. Dashing along a couple of corridors, I skidded around the final corner just in time to see Alex's kilt disappearing into the General's office. Assuming that Alex was inside his kilt, I could do nothing but eavesdrop on their conversation from outside the open door.

'Ah, Alexsh – whatsh up?'

'Here you are, General, as you requested.'

'What the devil is thish?'

'Er … it's the guest list you asked me for, Sir. Just now. On the phone.'

'I did no shuch thing. I'm busy here writing an important shpeesh. I think itsh a shet-up. You've been had, my good man.'

'Oh. Sorry, Sir.'

Clearly bemused, Alex wandered out of the General's office and immediately met my sheepish, apologetic grin.

'Charles Ritchie – I might have known! What the hell were you thinking?'

'Alex, I am sorry, but I really wanted those tickets.'

'I told you already, I haven't got any spare. Now leave me alone!'

I suddenly had one of my rare brainwaves, which briefly made me feel dizzy. Leaning against the wall to stop myself toppling over with smugness, I explained the situation to poor Alex.

'Listen here, my good fellow. If you get me those tickets, I promise to never, ever trick you again. But if you don't, then from now on, when the General phones you up, you will never know whether it's him or me on the other end.'

There was a pause while Alex digested the awfulness of this threat.

'You bastard, Charles.'

My parents thoroughly enjoyed the Mayor's reception.

*   *   *

Covert operations in East Germany occasionally involved hunkering down in woods near to the target site. Under cover of darkness, we would park the car up and pitch rain-sheets to keep us dry and allow a little sleep, before moving on at first light.

One operation involved monitoring a Soviet Army chemical weapons exercise, to try to discover the nature of the substances being used. We had learnt where and when the exercise was due to take place, through interception of radio communications, and had been given very strict and precise instructions. I went out the night before, with driver and NCO as usual, we hid the car and, forgoing our usual rain-sheets, we settled into a well-hidden observation site for the remainder of the night.

During the following morning, we watched through our binoculars as two archways were constructed, one on either side of the training site, tall and wide enough for large vehicles to drive through. Different vehicle types – a heavy tank, a light tank, a missile launcher, a heavy lorry, a light lorry, an APC, and so on – were driven through each archway and sprayed with a liquid. Clearly, the first archway was deploying some form of chemical weapon substance and the second archway was then deploying a decontaminant. There was perhaps 600 yards between the two archways – so pity the poor soldiers who had to drive all the way across to the second archway while exposed to whatever had been sprayed on their vehicle.

We watched this scenario play out until all the vehicles had left and the archways had been dismantled and removed.

Once the area was clear, I went to work to carry out my instructions. Wearing long plastic gloves, plastic leggings and a face-mask, I made my way over to where the first archway had been constructed and, using a trowel, dug up some earth that would have been exposed to the contaminant, placed the earth and the trowel in a plastic bag, sealed it and took it back to the car. Then, with fresh protective clothing and a fresh trowel, I proceeded to the decontamination area and collected earth from there, which I then sealed in a second plastic bag.

Our return to base was untroubled, and I duly delivered my two plastic bags. It was a couple of weeks later that it was confirmed that the materials we had gathered had proved very useful to our technical boffins in learning how to deal with a potential chemical weapon attack by the Soviets. The exercise had indeed used a chemical agent, albeit at what I was told was only 5 per cent strength, although the decontaminant agent used had been full-strength.

I'm glad to say that my exposure those many years ago to a chemical weapon seems to have caused me no lasting damage – unless the

Soviet plan was to bring down the West by contaminating us with an unquenchable thirst for rosé wine and nature documentaries.

* * *

In my BRIXMIS role I occasionally had to visit Spandau prison, located in the British sector of West Berlin. I therefore had several opportunities to talk to its one occupant, Rudolf Hess. The topics of conversation were many and varied, and I found Hess to be a thoughtful and unassuming man, although inevitably quite institutionalized by his long imprisonment.

One unexpected consequence of my visits to Spandau was of benefit to the British film industry. *The Wild Geese* had been a very successful film, made in 1978, about a group of British mercenaries hired to rescue a deposed African president from the hands of a corrupt dictator. It was based on a novel by Daniel Carney, and the screenplay was written by Reginald Rose.

Reginald was a great friend of Captain Piers Wedgwood of The Royal Scots. I had first met Piers when he was an officer cadet at Sandhurst. The year after *The Wild Geese* was released, Reginald came to visit Piers in Berlin as he had another novel by Daniel Carney which he wanted to convert into a screenplay. This was a follow-up to *The Wild Geese* in which the British mercenaries are hired to spring Rudolf Hess from Spandau prison, and Reginald had come to Piers to learn as much as possible about Spandau and what realistic ways there might be of getting its one inmate out.

Piers knew that in my BRIXMIS role I occasionally visited Spandau. I knew the layout of the prison and the nature of the prison security provided by the Army. I could therefore be a very useful source of information. Piers also knew of my love for the theatre and acting, so the chance to be involved in any way in the making of a major movie would appeal to me greatly and perhaps, hinted Piers, override my sense of duty, security and confidentiality?

Did it ever.

I sat down like an eager schoolboy with Piers and Reginald and basically told them exactly how Rudolf Hess could be sprung out of Spandau, and then out of West Berlin. Reginald made copious notes. Subject to a few subsequent alterations and additions, for dramatic effect and so on, the screenplay for the imaginatively-named *Wild Geese II*, starring Laurence Oliver and Edward Fox, was in some substantial part created from the loose-lipped, over-enthusiastic gossiping of an irresponsible young British Army Major.

*   *   *

In general terms, the East Germans hated the Russians, who were quite foul to them. Many East Germans were also firmly anti-communist. We were therefore able to develop very good relationships with some locals which occasionally proved very helpful.

One chap lived in a small house next to a major railway line, where he operated the level crossing gates. In exchange for a variety of Western goodies such as Nescafé and chocolate biscuits, he would flash a torch for us whenever we were parked up some distance from the line, to warn that there was a military train coming. We could then drive up to the crossing just in time to be stopped by the barriers right at the front, which was an ideal spot from which to record all the visible contents of the train as it trundled by.

I was once staying at the Hotel Elephant in Weimar during a town tour when we received an unexpected gift. As we were leaving, the hotel manager called me over and quietly handed over a small bag containing several rolls of exposed film.

'Major – please take these. We had a very charming RAF officer staying here last year and he accidentally left these behind under his pillow.'

There were sixteen rolls of film in total. Once back at HQ, we checked our records and located the RAF officer, who was still serving in the Mission. He had obviously reported the loss of the film in his tour report and was delighted they had been recovered without anything untoward happening. The films were all developed, although I have no idea of the value of what they contained, but our friendly hotel manager had obviously taken quite some risk in holding on to them.

*   *   *

While in West Berlin I was allowed to live in one of the MoD apartment blocks about a mile from BRIXMIS HQ. The block contained eight individual flats and, fortunately for me as a bachelor at a time, six of the other flats were occupied by delightful young women who taught at the local British Army Primary school across from the apartment block. The last flat was taken by a chap who worked for the NAAFI – Navy, Army and Air Force Institute, although people whose military career led them to the NAAFI were teased that it stood for 'No Ambition And F***-all Interest'.

I got on very well with the young teachers, who occasionally needed some practical help with something or other in their flats. One of them also managed to get me introduced to David Bowie. She tipped me off that he was living in Berlin at the time and paying substantial sums of money to have his son Zowie attend the British Army Primary School. He would occasionally do the school run, picking his son up from school at 4.00pm to take him back to his own apartment across town.

As the school was only yards from where I lived, I managed to 'accidentally' bump into the star a couple of times outside the school, and we got chatting. I invited him to a party at the Officers' Mess and was delighted when he showed up. To be honest, he didn't seem to enjoy himself very much, as there were too many star-struck guests making a nuisance of themselves.

However, he obviously appreciated the gesture and was a true gentleman because, in return, he invited me to a party held in his luxury apartment downtown. Now that was a party! The guests were all served incredible food and drink, and the host clearly felt he could relax in his own environment. As the evening wore on, David introduced me to a major record producer. I happened to ask him what he did with all the records that he must get sent.

'Oh, we get so many, we try to give them all away.'

'Really? I'd love to get some to take across to East Germany. The youngsters there cannot get their hands on any music from the West.'

'No problem!'

From then on, every few weeks, a pile of singles and albums was delivered to our HQ in West Berlin. Immune from any custom checks, I would take them across the border into East Germany and give them away to local East Germans as a gesture of goodwill, courtesy of David Bowie and friends.

*   *   *

I was on weekend duty at the Mission House in Potsdam. We took turns in running the house at weekends to allow the Sergeant Major and his wife, who were there throughout the week, to spend their weekends in Berlin.

I was having a quiet day when I received a phone call from my Russian counterpart.

'Major Ritchie, we have a problem. We have got two of your Scottish soldiers here in Potsdam.'

'What? That's not possible!'

But it was. Two young privates from The Royal Highland Fusiliers had been out on the town after finishing a skiing training course in Bavaria with the rest of their platoon. After getting very drunk they had got into a punch-up with a West German pub owner and been placed under close arrest for the night.

Expecting to be charged in the morning, our intrepid Jocks had decided to go AWOL by trying to cross *into* East Germany *from* West Germany, and had been caught in the 'dog run', having scaled the fence and somehow wandered safely through the minefield! Not knowing what to do with them, the East Germans handed them over to the Russians – hence the call to me.

I jumped in the car along with my driver for the day, Corporal Byers, and we drove down to SERB HQ, where the two rascals were being held. After hearing the story again from my Russian colleagues, I asked how the runaways had managed to avoid the anti-personnel mines, but the Russians were as bemused as the Germans had been.

I asked to see the culprits and was duly led down to their cell. However, I was dressed in civvies, and when I introduced myself to the beleaguered pair, they were very jumpy and suspicious.

'Ach, yer no' a Scottish Major, yer havin' us oan.'

'I can assure you, I am Major Ritchie of The Royal Scots and I'm here to help you.'

'The Royal Scots, eh? Gonnae show us yer ID then?'

That was tricky, because while in East Germany I only had my Soviet Army ID card, as my British Army ID card was held at the checkpoint on the Glienicke Bridge. I tried to explain this to them, but of course it made them even more suspicious.

'Okay, if yer Scottish then – wha's the cap'n o'Glesga Rangers fitba' team?'

'I have no idea.'

'Wha' aboot Celtic, then?'

'Not the foggiest, sorry.'

My ignorance of Scottish football was highly suspicious to the two young Fusiliers but, thankfully, Corporal Byers came to my rescue. In his broad Glaswegian accent, he gave the two youngsters a right rollocking, explained who I was, how much shit they were in, and that they had better shape up. That did the trick. He also told them I was a Partick Thistle supporter and so clearly knew nothing about football.

I signed some paperwork to allow the Russians to release the pair into our custody, together with a special pass to allow us to get them back into West Berlin.

While we were waiting for Corporal Byers to fetch the car, I asked the two of them about their highly unusual attempt at crossing the infamous border in the wrong direction.

'Tell me, lads – I understand how you got over the fence, given that it's designed to stop people coming the other way. But how did you get through the anti-personnel minefield?'

'Dunno, Sir. But we wuz still so pished, we couldna walk straight. We wuz weaving aboot all o'er the place among yon straight lines the Germans love, mebbe that did the trick?'

I've had a few lucky escapes in my time, but that one took the biscuit.

* * *

The Girl Guide movement in Germany was holding a Weekend for Guide Leaders in West Berlin. BRIXMIS was contacted for help, and I was roped in to give a practical course to the Guide Leaders on 'How to Cope in Extreme Weather Conditions', during which I taught them how to stay warm, how to build temporary shelters and the like. Most of the Guiders were capable young women, but I was surprised to meet a few who were rather arrogant and seriously incompetent.

When the event was over, a dinner was hosted by the Berlin Commissioner for Guides, a wonderful woman called Gillian Scott-Forrest, for all the people who had helped with the weekend. During the dinner I was asked what I thought of the Guiders I had met. I gave an honest appraisal, which did include the fact that I thought two of the group were pretty hopeless; I expressed concern that, if either of them were left alone with a Guide troop in poor weather conditions, they could all be dead by morning.

This caused quite some consternation around the dinner table, with comments to the effect that it was very hard to encourage young women to become Guiders, it was a very broad-ranging and difficult role and perhaps I should 'try it some time'.

That was a challenge I could not refuse.

'OK – I would genuinely like to become a Guider. I think I would be very good at it. How do I apply?'

'Oh, but Major Ritchie – you know we only have female Guiders. Men are not allowed.'

'Really? I assure I am very well qualified to be a leader. There are female cub leaders – why can't you have a male guide leader?'

'Oh, come now, Major, you are not serious now, are you?'

'If you don't allow me to apply, you will be in breach of the European Union Convention on Human Rights.'

I had no idea if that was true, but it certainly put the cat among the pigeons and a fox in the henhouse.

Things happened surprisingly quickly in the days following that dinner, culminating in my being invited to an interview one Sunday morning in the local Girl Guide hall, in front of Gillian and a number of other Guide Commissioners, two of whom had been flown in especially from London.

During the interview I was asked multiple questions, in a rather tangential way, about why I wanted to be a Guider and whether it was related to any sexual proclivities. They even tackled me on what I would wear – insisting that the Guider uniform included a blue skirt. I told them that as a Scot I was very comfortable wearing a kilt and so it would not be a problem.

Eventually, they ran out of ideas on how to get me to back down, and the interview was terminated. Gillian came to see me immediately afterwards.

'Charles – please – I'm begging you. You have to help us out of this. We obviously cannot be seen to publicly reject your application …'

I felt the whole thing had gone far enough. My point had been made.

'Ok, Gillian, I'll get you off the hook. The one question you have not asked is whether I am able to commit to the time required to be a Guider, i.e. every Thursday evening and one weekend a month. As a member of BRIXMIS, I cannot possible guarantee that availability – I could be sent to East Germany at short notice.'

'So … you will rescind your application?'

'No. I want you to accept my application and make me a Guider. I give you my word that I will then immediately resign, due to being unable to commit to the time required.'

And that is what happened. There was a short welcoming ceremony, I was presented with my Guider's Badge and I made a short thank-you speech of acceptance, then promptly announced my resignation. The sighs of relief around the room were deafening. But I do believe I was the very first ever official male Guider of the Girl Guide movement.

*   *   *

One of the most successful intelligence-gathering operations in which I took part involved the Soviets' new T80 tank, which had revolutionary technology such as Explosive Reactive Armour, offering much greater protection against anti-tank ordnance.

We discovered that a group of these new tanks had arrived at the barracks of the Russian's 16th Guards Tank Division stationed in Ludwiglust, north-west of Berlin. Fortunately, their arrival coincided with a scheduled 'rotation', whereby 25 per cent of the Russian military personnel would be rotated out and returned to the motherland, having completed their two-year tour. The two-week periods around a barracks rotation were prime times for us, as security was more lax than usual, with guards who were either looking forward to going home so not concentrating, or who had just arrived at the start of their tour and didn't know what they were doing.

We drove up to Ludwiglust one evening and chose a spot on the training area about a mile from the back gate of the barracks, where we let our car get stuck (in two-wheel drive mode) in some mud at the side of a track. At around 3.30am, leaving the driver with the car, the Sergeant and I set off to 'get help'. We cautiously approached the barracks and were delighted to see that the sentry towers were unoccupied.

The rear gate was chained but not padlocked. While the Sergeant kept a look-out, I slipped through the gate and made my way to the main HQ building. I tried a few windows at the side of the building and, finding one that opened, clambered in and made my way around the corridors, trying various office doors and generally looking for anything interesting. The place was pretty deserted, and I only had to hide a couple of times as footsteps passed nearby, but as I ducked from room to room my heart was in my mouth and my brain was screaming at me to scarper.

I finally hit the jackpot in one large office. Lying on the desk was a small pile of what I recognized as confidential Russian military documents, although I could not read what they said. I took one document at random and stuffed it up my jumper. The golden rule was to take only one document, never more – a document going missing is usually assumed to have been lost or mislaid, whereas if several documents vanish, it alerts the owners to something more serious.

My exit from the barracks was as remarkably untroubled as my entry, and the Sergeant and I hurried back to the car, where our driver was waiting. He promptly engaged four-wheel drive and we drove off. Once we were safely back on the main road, the Sergeant asked the obvious question.

'So, Sir – what have you got?'

'I have absolutely no idea.'

I pulled the document out from under my jumper. It looked interesting – but it was not until the debrief from our technical officer in West Berlin, a chap called Ian Mercer, that we discovered I had somehow managed to snatch a copy of the main technical specification for the T80 tank itself. It was promptly shipped back to the Ministry of Defence in London, and copies were provided to the French, the Americans and the West Germans.

As a result of the Soviets' introduction of the ground-breaking T80, and what we subsequently learnt about it, a new generation of upgraded battle tanks had to be produced by various NATO countries, including the British Challenger 2, the American M1 Abrams, the French Leclerc and the West German Leopard 2.

My night out in Ludwiglust may have indirectly cost NATO countries over £100 billion in additional military defence expenditure. Oops.

*   *   *

During the Cold War years, the Warsaw Pact countries held a major annual military exercise, partly as a show of strength, partly to galvanize their political forces. This was held in a different location each year, and always included a major parade, with great ceremony and speeches from the top brass. In German this was a 'Waffenbruderschaft', which loosely translated means 'Brothers-in-arms'. In 1980, the Waffenbruderschaft ceremony was held in Potsdam.

BRIXMIS and our allies were obviously on high alert to try to monitor the military exercise themselves, but the possibility of gatecrashing the opening ceremony itself, right on our doorstep, was an opportunity not to be missed.

I was with Sergeant Ray MacDonald from the Royal Scots Dragoon Guards, whose berets look very similar to those of the Polish Army – blue, with a cap badge that looks like the Polish Army dragon. On the day of the ceremony, we strode down to the town centre, both wearing Guards berets as I had somehow conveniently forgotten my own tam-o'-shanter. We knew full well that, although we were legitimately dressed, we looked at first glance like members of the Polish Army.

The edge of the town square was heaving with Warsaw Pact military of all types trying to get themselves organized in their rightful positions. When we got to the barriers, a Russian officer took one glance at us, as we held our breath.

'Polski …?'

We simply nodded, and he directed us to the Polish Army sector. However, the Poles, to our consternation, had been positioned right in front of the main stage. So much for hiding away in a quiet corner to view the proceedings – we were no more than 15ft from the stage. Nevertheless, nodding politely, we lined up next to our new Polish colleagues and waited for the dignitaries to arrive.

Eventually, to a musical fanfare, the great and good of the Warsaw Pact walked out, including Erich Honecker, General Secretary of the Socialist Party in East Germany, and Colonel General Grinkevitch, then commander of the Soviet Army in East Germany, whom I had met several times previously.

As Herr Honecker rose to give his welcoming speech, I unfortunately caught the eye of the Colonel General, who did a comedy double-take in shock at recognizing my boyish good looks shining out from the front row of the massed Warsaw Pact military machine. Quickly regaining his composure, he fixed me with a cold hard stare, pointed an accusing finger and mouthed something in Russian which I assumed was not 'Have a nice day'.

On Monday morning, unsurprisingly, I received the call that the Colonel General wanted to see me, so I went along with an interpreter and a member of SERB. We were duly marched into his office, where the conversation through the interpreter was rather entertaining.

'Major Ritchie – what the hell were you doing at the Waffenbruderschaft ceremony!?'

'Well, Sir, if I tell you, you probably won't believe me.

'Correct. I won't!'

'Well, we went shopping, but in the town centre there was obviously a big parade or something going on. A nice Russian officer directed us, and we found ourselves accidentally at the front of the crowd, next to some Polish Army chaps.'

'Why in hell would one of my officers direct you into the ceremony?'

'Ah, well, you see, Sir, I had forgotten my own headgear so had borrowed one from my Sergeant. His grey beret and cap badge do look terribly similar to those of the Polish Army, and I think it was an honest mistake by your officer ...'

I waited for the next assault, but instead there was an interminable silence, before the Colonel General stood up and opened a drawer in his desk. I thought for a split second he was going to pull out a revolver, such was his apparent fury. That would have been quite a severe punishment, I felt, although maybe a game of Russian roulette would have been more in keeping ...

However, as he took a small box from his desk his whole demeanour changed, and I saw the glimmer of a wry smile.

'Major Ritchie – whether I like it or not, you attended the grand opening ceremony of the Waffenbruderschaft. All attending officers receive a medal of commemoration, so here is yours. Now, get out of my sight.'

I have the medal to this day.

*   *   *

I was asked to attend a meeting with an MI6 officer at their HQ in West Berlin.

'Charles – I understand you are to be the duty officer in Potsdam next weekend?'

'Yes, correct.'

'Tell me, what do you usually do when you are there?'

'Well, I spend the weekend in the house. The only time I go out is once the Sergeant Major returns on Sunday evening, when I take the opportunity to visit a particular bar located between a Russian barracks and an East German barracks.'

'Why do you go there, Charles?'

'Well, it's always full of Russian and East German officers, and we have a budget to buy drinks for them, to keep them chummy. They know us quite well, and you never know when such bonhomie might lead to something useful.'

'How long do you stay in the bar?'

'We only stay about an hour, say our farewells to firm handshakes and slaps on the back, and then drive back to the Mission House, where I say goodbye to the staff, grab my bag and head off back to West Berlin.'

There was a long pause while my friendly interrogator furrowed his brow. He was clearly pondering a decision, but finally he spoke again.

'Okay, Charles, on next weekend's visit to the pub, I want you to do exactly as I say …'

He then brought out an aerial photograph of the area around the pub in Potsdam. Clearly, he had already been well briefed about my Sunday evening habits. He proceeded to give me strict instructions for my next visit which I was to follow to the letter.

That weekend in Potsdam, after an uneventful stay at the Mission House, the duty driver and I took our usual route in the Mission car down to the bar. As instructed, we parked in the side street, left the car unlocked and proceeded into the bar, where I bought drinks as usual for all the Soviet and East German officers there.

However, at 6.45pm precisely, earlier than usual, I made my excuses involving something about a dinner party in West Berlin, left a sizeable tab at the bar to allow the drinking to continue in my absence, and we drove back to the Mission House so I could say my goodbyes and get my bag, which I had been instructed to simply throw on the back seat of the car. I guessed that I was being used as a mule for a parcel, which presumably had been put in the unlocked boot of the car while we had been buying drinks.

My driver and I then set off for the Glienicke bridge, our usual crossing point between Potsdam and West Berlin. However, as we approached the bridge we suddenly heard a distinct cough from the boot of the car – quite high-pitched, like that of a child. I glanced at my driver, who returned a look of astonishment. I signalled to him to keep driving towards the barriers, while I quickly turned and in my best German gave a quick instruction.

'Be very quiet for the next ten minutes – we are just 400 metres from the Glienicke Bridge.'

We came on to the bridge and entered the steel-gated 'cage', where a very bored-looking Russian sentry took our ID cards and the official car pass. He then walked slowly around the car, banging occasionally on the roof, the doors, and the boot – standard practice, but in this instance quite unnerving. Eventually, he exchanged our paperwork, waved to the gate operator and directed us on our way.

We drove across the halfway mark on the bridge which denoted the border into West Berlin. I then turned around in my seat and spoke again in German.

'Don't worry. We are now safely in West Berlin.'

There was a sob from the boot of the car and we heard an adult male voice, charged with emotion.

'Vielen, vielen dank!' [Thank you very, very much].

We drove to our military base in the West Berlin Olympic Stadium, parked the car where instructed, grabbed our bags from the back seat and walked away.

The next morning, I was sent for by the MI6 chap, who warmly shook my hand as soon as I stepped into his office.

'Charles – well done!'

'You *bastard*, you should have told me!'

'Sorry, Charles, but it was for your own safety. What you did last night had to have the personal authority of the Prime Minister.'

'Who the hell was in the boot of my car?'

'My dear chap – you will never know.'

There was then a formal debrief, at which I again asked who had been in the boot of the car, and again was told that I was never to know.

I regret to this day not opening the boot after we had parked at the base, so that I could come face-to-face with whomever we had spirited across the border. It would have been against orders, but I could have claimed concern for the safety of my illicit passengers.

Anyway, I would still love to know, even now.

*   *   *

My posting to BRIXMIS came to a premature end, three months before my two-year stint was due to complete, when I broke the Eleventh Commandment – 'Thou shall not get caught'.

It was during what started off as a routine intelligence-gathering outing. Acting on a tip-off that some interesting activity was imminent, we had gone out during the night to set up at an observation point close to a Russian Army training area. Our driver stayed with the car, parked well away, while the Sergeant and I made ourselves comfortable amongst a dense clump of bushes and got our camera gear and audio equipment ready. We had to be well hidden as we never wore camouflage uniforms – we were dressed in our usual standard-issue khaki trousers, shirt and pullover, with a small BRIXMIS badge sewn on to the pullover, but no cap badge for fear of torchlight reflection giving us away.

At dawn, a family of wild boar wandered past, so I took a couple of pictures. It was always good to have some wildlife shots in the film, as a potential alibi.

A short while later, we heard the rumble of approaching vehicles, and our tip-off seemed to be on the money, for along came a convoy of two dozen 'GAZ-66' trucks – standard Russian lightweight trucks, so not interesting in themselves, but what they were carrying was different. Each lorry was fitted with a type of surface-to-surface missile launcher that we had never seen before, but which we later learned was Russia's first nuclear-capable 'air-portable' system, i.e. able to be transported in a military cargo plane.

As the convoy rolled past, I shot a whole roll of film, while the Sergeant recorded all the registration numbers of the vehicles. Once the dust had settled (literally), we emerged from our hiding place and headed back to the car.

We were only a few hundred yards from our vehicle when we were jumped by six camouflaged members of Spetznatz, the Russian equivalent of the British SAS, who were lying in wait for us. As per our standard procedures, I had not wound my camera film back fully into its reel, so that I could quickly pull the whole film out to destroy it by exposure. However, our assailants knew what they were doing – we were pinned to the ground within seconds, with no time to destroy the evidence. They duly retrieved my camera and film, along with the Sergeant's audio recording tape.

We were frog-marched back to our car, where our driver was sat with a rifle pointed at his head. We had all been arrested several times before, but only as part of the usual 'nuisance' tactics, when the charges were trumped-up or non-existent. This was different – we knew we were in a spot of bother.

A Russian officer asked for our identity cards, which we handed over. We were then left standing at rifle-point for an age, until another officer approached me and spoke in English.

'Identity Card, please.'

'I've already given it to the other officer.'

'What other officer? I am the only officer here.'

I looked around. The Russian who had initially taken our identity cards had vanished.

'Er … there was another officer here earlier …'

'You are lying. You have no identity card. You are clearly a spy.'

With that, they pulled a sandbag sack over my head and threw me in the back of a truck, which set off down the forest track with me bouncing around on the floor and getting the occasional push or prod from the jeering Russian soldiers sat around me. I was reasonably confident that no great physical harm was going to come to me – at least, they would not do anything that would leave visible marks, to avoid the risk of the British making a claim of maltreatment or torture.

I was driven to an army barracks, taken into a room and placed in a chair. The sandbag was removed from my head. The English-speaking Russian officer was in front of me, with a few others milling around.

'Who are you?'

'I am Major Ritchie of the British Army. I am a member of the British Military Liaison Mission, based in Potsdam.'

'Tell us what you were doing in the forest.'

'I was photographing wildlife.'

'Liar.'

'But I was. A lovely family of wild boar.'

'Huh. We are getting your camera film developed. We will soon see.'

After some more questioning and a bit of ranting and cursing at me, the interrogation paused for a while, until I was led into an adjoining room to be presented with the photographs from my camera, neatly laid out on a large table.

'Explain these.'

'Well, you can see from these first two, that I was indeed taking pictures of a group of wild boar. Then this line of forestry lorries drove along the track and blocked my view, presumably on their way to lay these new water pipes they are carrying.'

'Major Ritchie – you know perfectly well that these are missile launchers, not water pipes.'

'No! Really!?'

'Explain this photograph, where you have managed to take a close-up of the sighting system on one of these missile launchers!'

It was true. I momentarily flushed with pride, because on one exposure I had managed to get my 1,000mm lens focused precisely on the sighting system, which would have given our technical boffins a thrill if the photo had ever got back to them.

I paused to think of something intelligent to say. That failed, so I stuck to my guns.

'Well, I guess I was so annoyed at these forestry lorries getting in my way, I pressed the zoom button by mistake.'

My Russian host got a bit frustrated at this point, as he finally realized that I was going to hold firmly to my rather ridiculous storyline, irrespective of the evidence laid out in front of me.

After some more rather half-hearted interrogation, I was taken to see a medic and examined, to provide independent evidence that I had not been beaten up. I was then taken outside to our car. My colleagues had been allowed to follow the truck I was in, although they had not been allowed to enter the Russian army barracks and so had been parked outside this whole time, wondering what the Russians were doing with me.

The three of us were then escorted to the Glienicke Bridge and sent back into West Berlin.

Over the next few days there was a political hoo-hah, in which my boss was told by the Russians what they claimed I had done, and he duly claimed I must be innocent and there must be some mix-up, etc., etc. The final result was that the Russians formally announced that I was no longer welcome as part of the British Military Mission. The exact words were as follows:

> Major Ritchie's secret actions have made him incompatible to continue as a member of the British Military Liaison Mission.

*   *   *

Despite being *persona non grata* in East Germany, I was invited to a farewell party hosted by the Russians at their Officers' Club in Potsdam. It was a lovely evening, topped off by a very nice little speech given by Colonel General Grinkevitch.

'Major Ritchie – we are here tonight to say farewell. I would like to say three things. One – we have all enjoyed your company.'

There were cheers around the room, which made me blush.

'Two – despite recent difficulties, we congratulate you on your promotion to Lieutenant Colonel and your new Battalion command in Northern Ireland.'

With the exception of my boss, this was news to all the British officers present. I have no idea how the Russians got to hear of it.

'And three – we would like to present you with a small gift to commemorate your time with us.'

With that, he snapped his fingers and a guard appeared with a silver tray on which was a Soviet officer's winter fur hat.

'Major Ritchie, in presenting you with this gift, and speaking on behalf of every Soviet Officer here tonight – we are all delighted and relieved that you are leaving!'

It was a touching gesture from a genuine soldier and gentleman.

*   *   *

As a result of my endeavours in Berlin and East Germany, I was awarded a Guider's badge, a Russian officer's fur hat and an MBE.

I was honoured to receive the MBE at Buckingham Palace from Her Majesty the Queen. I suspect that someone close to Her Majesty may have had a few words in advance, because I was rather chuffed with the personal comment as I was presented with my medal.

'Major Ritchie, I read your citation with great interest. This may be the first time I have awarded an MBE for stealing!'

I just grinned like a fool and concentrated on not falling over.

Chapter 10

Thou Art Mad; Get Thee a Wife

On returning to the UK from Berlin, I took up my posting in Northern Ireland as a Lieutenant Colonel commanding the 3rd Battalion Ulster Defence Regiment (UDR).

In a similar fashion to the Territorial Army in the rest of the UK, it was general practice for regular army officers from other regiments to command the mostly part-time UDR. Coincidentally, the house provided to me as Commanding Officer was right next door to the CO's house of The Royal Scots, who were based next to us in Ballykinler.

It was a little strange being in charge of another battalion while being so close to my own regiment. However, the men and women of the UDR were absolutely wonderful to work with, and I made some truly great friends.

*   *   *

As a Commanding Officer I always liked to get a sense for what the men under my command faced on a day-to-day basis. While in Northern Ireland, I occasionally dressed as a private UDR soldier and took part for a few hours in a road-block duty or some such task. However, my hands-on approach was slightly hampered by the fact that the men of the UDR were obviously all Irish, with accents to match, whereas my anglicized Scotch brogue stood out like a sore thumb.

Attending road-block duty one day, I dusted off my best Northern Ireland accent, as employed by my alter ego from Bessbrook Mill, the outrageous Major Loyalty McFriland. The idea was to try it out on the local community rather than simply as clownish entertainment for my colleagues. I had fooled Italians, Arabs, Russians and Germans with my skill at accents and so was confident I could carry this off without anyone noticing.

I stopped the first car that approached the road-block, fresh in my UDR private's uniform, watched with some amusement by the soldiers under my command. Stepping up to the driver's door, I issued my instructions.

''Scuse me, mistor – wid ye mind put'n yer lights out, an' moving down the road thar, whar ye see the man wi' the green light?'

The good local responded enthusiastically.

'Aye, ah'll do tha fer ye, son … an tell me this, whit part o' Englind err you fraum?'

I withdrew, blushing, and left my men to their work.

*   *   *

The single most memorable event during my second tour happened one evening as I was touring around County Down, inspecting the road-blocks that we had in place throughout the county.

Approaching a T-junction where one of our road-blocks had been established, we saw a car parked on the side of the road, perhaps no more than 200 yards from the troops up ahead. This was obviously very suspicious. We pulled up behind the car, and RSM Duffus and I got out, pulled our pistols and approached either side of the vehicle.

We discovered that the gentleman in the driver's seat and the lady with him were, to put it mildly, not fully clothed. But before we could recover our composure and they could gather their underwear, a huge German Shepherd dog came bounding out of the farm entrance on the opposite side of the road, barking angrily. It went straight for the RSM, leapt up at him and sank its teeth into his outstretched arm.

The RSM yelled in pain and surprise. I rushed around the car and without hesitation shot the dog through the neck, killing it instantly. I could have also injured the RSM as the bullet passed straight through the dog, but fortunately it missed him. Less fortunately, the bullet continued on its way down the road towards the roadblock and gently pinged off one of the army vehicles.

Thinking they were under attack, the soldiers at the road-block immediately prepared to return fire and were only stopped by the quick thinking of our driver, who had remained in the car watching this scene unfold. He immediately yelled down the radio to warn them who we were.

Having narrowly escaped being shot at by our own men, I turned my attention to the farmhouse from which the dog had appeared. The farmer, clearly the worse for drink, was now leaning out of an upstairs bedroom window, regaling us with his best Irish curses for having shot his poor dog.

Arguably worse news was to follow for the farmer. On questioning the couple in the car, it transpired that the lady was in fact the farmer's wife and the driver was an (extremely) friendly neighbour. She had plied her husband with drink and put him to bed, in order to have a clandestine meeting with her lover. Unfortunately, their ardour was such that they hadn't even waited to drive away from the house, hence the compromised position we had found them in when we first arrived.

I enjoyed writing the police report on the evening's events – I wish I had kept a copy for posterity. However, I did receive a very nice letter from Sir John 'Jack' Hermon, the Chief Constable of the Royal Ulster Constabulary (RUC). I had not expected my report to end up on the Chief Constable's desk, but obviously someone at HQ thought it worthy of his attention.

Sir John's letter was short and sweet. It read as follows.

Dear Colonel Ritchie,
I would like to thank you for submitting what has to be the funniest situation report I have ever seen in my 30 years of policing.
Yours etc

*   *   *

I have been accused of many things in my career, but only once of cheating. The accusers were none other than The Pony Club.

There was a big Pony Club tetrathlon competition to be held in County Down, hosted by the local branch run by Val Campbell, the wife of a good army friend. Val twisted my arm to take over from an ex-cavalry officer in training the boys. I've never mastered horse-riding – it's true that the hardest thing about learning to ride a horse is the ground. But I could definitely help the boys with the other disciplines of running, shooting and swimming. In particular, the Army had a first-class indoor shooting range at Ballykinler, and so I was able to organize regular shooting practice for the boys, under the guidance of our best instructors.

On the day of the competition, our local lads swept the board during the shooting event in such convincing fashion that suspicious questions were asked of them. They proudly explained how they had been taught at the British Army range under the guidance of Colonel Ritchie and his instructors.

There followed a formal letter of complaint from Pony Club HQ in England, accusing me of cheating by employing professional assistance for a Pony Club event. Very competitive, these horsey types!

* * *

I often dined in the local restaurants around County Down, employing a driver to take me there and home again. However, one evening I had a rebellious rush of blood to the head and decided I would drive myself out to dinner. I went to a restaurant in Ballynahinch and had such a good meal that I simply forgot that I had to drive home afterwards.

Feeling a little too jolly for my own good, I confidently set off. The journey was mostly uneventful, although I did swerve violently to miss a tree, before realizing it was the air-freshener hanging from the rear-view mirror.

As I weaved my way into Ballykinlar, I saw an RUC road-block ahead of me. They would almost certainly want to search the car but, if they suspected anything dodgy, they could also breathalyse the driver.

I quickly pulled over and grabbed the radio.

'Hello Zero, this is Nine.'

'Go ahead, Nine – this is Zero.'

'In exactly thirty seconds' time, radio me an urgent message to return to your Ops location immediately.'

I then drove slowly down to the checkpoint, mentally counting out the seconds in my head. I was met by a smart young RUC officer, who recognized me as I handed over my identity card.

'Oh, hello, Sir. Er ... mind if we check your vehicle?'

'Not at all, young man.'

At that precise moment, my radio burst into life.

'Hello Nine, this is Zero.'

'Go ahead, Zero.'

'Urgent message. Return to base immediately. Repeat – return to base immediately!'

I looked up at the RUC officer with an apologetic shrug.

'Sorry, young man, but that sounds pretty important. May I dash?'

I was promptly waved through and, concentrating hard, drove back home safe and sound. Disgraceful behaviour and misuse of power, I know.

* * *

Sean Rafferty has worked at the BBC in Northern Ireland for ever. I got to know him while I was posted there – a wonderful chap.

Sean invited me and a lady friend to Belfast to attend a theatre show, followed by dinner. I lined up a charming date, put on my best civvies and drove to the theatre. After the show, and a wonderful dinner, I left the others having a final drink while I went to collect the car, which I had left in the theatre car park.

As I turned the corner into the now dark and empty car park, two very large local lads stepped out in front of me, blocking my way.

'Roight, mister – we don' want ony trouble – just han' o'er yer watch an' yer wallet.'

'Okay, fine, no trouble.'

I paused for a second's thought, then reached inside my jacket pocket. But instead of taking out my wallet, I pulled out my 9mm automatic pistol, which I always wore even when dressed in civilian clothes. I cocked it and pointed it at one of the man-mountains in front of me.

'See, it's no trouble, boys.'

It was their turn to pause.

'Ah, fer enough …'

And with a shrug of the shoulders, they turned and sauntered away.

* * *

I was in attendance at a regular road-block one day in the centre of Downpatrick. I was keeping my Northern Irish accent in check when who should drive up but a very well known member of the IRA. At least, he was well known to us, although we had nothing firm enough to arrest him on and so, at the time, he continued to come and go as he pleased, which we obviously found extremely frustrating.

I therefore took a snap decision to have some fun at his expense. As he wound down the window of his car, I sauntered up to him in my most jovial and gregarious fashion and greeted him by his first name, as one would greet a long-lost friend.

'Kenneth! How wonderful to see you again – you're looking grand!'

He stared at me, confused and obviously trying to place me, although we had never met before. I ploughed on with my game.

'It was SO good of you to help our lads out with all that information. SO helpful, really very useful indeed!'

My prey was transfixed, his mouth agape. A small crowd of locals were watching while my soldiers suppressed their sniggering. Eventually, he spluttered into action.

'Aye don't know onything abowt thus … I have no fockin' idea what yer talking abowt … shor I've nivver seen you before in me fockin' loif!'

I leaned back against his car door and gave a theatrical grin to the onlookers.

'Oh, come now, Kenneth – stop over-acting, will you!'

Steam was now blowing out of his ears as he frantically looked about him at the gathering locals. Some of them undoubtedly knew who he was and were becoming curious as to the warm welcome he was receiving from the UDR.

Things had gone far enough, and I decided to defuse the situation before it got out of control. I leaned into the car and spoke to him discreetly in my best military soft-but-firm voice.

'Lieutenant Colonel Ritchie, Commanding Officer, Ulster Defence Regiment. If we receive a useful piece of anonymous information in the next 24 hours, I give you my word I'll never do this to you again.'

With that, I stood back and waved him on.

The next morning, we happened to get an anonymous phone call informing us to where to find a sizeable stash of firearms and ammunition.

* * *

I was being driven back to HQ one late February afternoon. We had a 'Greenfinch' in the car – the nickname for a female RUC officer. As we drove along a quiet country road, I was snoozing, but she was on the ball.

She pointed out of the car window to a farm at the side of the road.

'Sir – that's curious. That silage pit hasn't been touched since it was filled last year. The feed should be well-used by now.'

I am no farmer, but I instantly knew what she was getting at. Who knew what could be hiding under the mass of tarpaulins and used tyres? Not cut grass, it would seem.

When we got back to HQ, I promptly organized a raid. A small army of UDR soldiers and RUC officers descended on the farm buildings and in particular the silage pit itself, which on closer inspection was soundly constructed with concrete walls and a locked and bolted doorway in the side.

The farmer was led out from the farmhouse, clearly in a state of shock at the sudden invasion of his quiet corner of the countryside. We asked him to unlock the side door of the silage pit, which he did with a shaking hand. He then led us into what I believe was the biggest and best poteen distillery ever discovered in Northern Ireland.

After having had a good look at the scale of the operation we had uncovered, I took the RUC commander to one side and we debated what to do. There was no way a bootleg operation of this scale was being carried out without the knowledge, and probable involvement, of the IRA. Being of similar mind, we agreed a plan and returned to the farmer, who was surprised to receive the offer of a get-out-of-jail free card – one significant piece of intelligence every month on IRA activity, and we would leave him and his poteen operation untouched.

That single decision, unconventional though it was, brought us a steady stream of valuable intelligence in the coming months. In one particular case it saved the lives of The Royal Scots pipe band, who had been targeted on their journey back from an Armistice Day parade with a culvert bomb placed under the road. The bomb was never detonated, thanks to the poteen distiller.

* * *

Towards the end of my second tour of Northern Ireland, The Royal Scots were due to celebrate their 350th anniversary, and a massive celebratory ball was organized back in Edinburgh, attended by a number of special guests, including Princess Anne as our Colonel in Chief.

All officers had a plus-one to invite. I was seeing a lovely Irish girl at the time. She was married but separated from her husband and was going through divorce proceedings. I therefore felt she needed some cheering up and so I invited her as my plus-one; it's not every day you get to sit at the same dinner table as a real live Princess.

She was delighted with the idea and got more and more excited as we planned our trip to Scotland in great detail. But a few days before the event, I happened to have a routine phone call with Lieutenant General Sir Bob Richardson, Colonel of the Regiment, and he asked whom I was taking as my plus-one. When I told him, there was a pregnant pause at the other end of the phone before he spoke again.

'Now, Charles, you know that's not on, dear boy.'

'Why ever not, Sir?'

'Well, dammit – we can't have an officer of The Royal Scots bringing someone else's wife to the top table at such an event. Just not the thing at all. You'll need to make an excuse and find someone else.'

And that was it. There was no point in arguing, but it cost me my relationship with my Irish girlfriend, as she would have nothing more to do with me after that.

As I scoured my list of acquaintances for someone suitable to invite, I remembered Araminta Luard. I had only met her a few times, but she was great fun and extremely attractive. As a bonus, she was living in Edinburgh at the time so would save me a bundle on travel expenses.

I called her up with the invitation and she graciously accepted, although she did need a bit of convincing. She confessed during the ball that she had thought from our previous meetings that I was a bit of an ass, so I marked her down not only as fun and attractive but also an excellent judge of character. Marriage material, clearly.

Indeed, we wed the very next year.

* * *

My next posting was as a member of the Directing Staff at the Joint Services Defence College at Greenwich, London. The purpose of this College is to give officers from across the three services a wider level of training and experience that encompasses multi-service operations.

I had a shaky start on day one when I was sent to meet the Senior Directing Staff officer. There was no name on his door, and as I marched into his office and stood to attention in front of his desk, my new boss was looking out of the window. I recognized the uniform of the Paras as he turned to me and spoke.

'Ah – if I'm not mistaken, it's Major Loyalty MacFriland of 12 UDR!'

My new boss was none other than Colonel Peter Morton, who had been on the receiving end of my clowning act back in Bessbrook Mill. I was, unusually for me, temporarily lost for words, my jaw hanging loose, expecting some backlash. Thankfully, he shook my hand warmly and grinned.

I spent two years in Greenwich, with Peter as my boss. We got on very well, and I enjoyed the job, although in all honesty it was not desperately exciting.

*   *   *

Due to a shortage of bachelor accommodation at Greenwich, I moved into married quarters in the main building, sharing the flat with a Royal Marine Lieutenant Colonel called Richard Persse. Richard lived in Portsmouth with his wife and children, so while he was working in Greenwich he commuted up to London on a Monday, stayed in the flat for four nights, then went home on Friday.

We each had a bedroom and bathroom and we shared the enormous drawing room where you could easily have eighty people for drinks. We also had a dining room in which you could comfortably have sixteen sitting down for dinner. All our meals were supplied in the dining room in the Great Hall, and I had a huge apartment to myself over the weekends – so it was a good life.

It was while I was based in Greenwich that Araminta and I got married. We were given permission to have the wedding service in the College's beautiful chapel, followed by a reception in the Officers' Mess, which was directly below the chapel. We decided to be dressed in civvies rather than have myself and most of the guests in military uniform. However, as a nod to my regiment, the page boys and bridesmaids all had outfits made in The Royal Scots regimental tartan.

*   *   *

Once Araminta and I had returned from our honeymoon in Amalfi to the Greenwich flat, Richard kindly moved out of his double bedroom into my old single room, although we had to get used to married life with him as a sort of lodger during the week. But it was fine – we got on very well. Araminta would cook him breakfast in the morning, and he would dine in the evening in the Officers' Mess.

It was more of a problem with Chrissie, our housekeeper. As single 'livers-in', Richard and I had the services of a housekeeper to clean the flat, change our bed linen, clean our shoes, etc. The first night we were back from honeymoon, as was my habit, I put my shoes outside the door as did Richard, for Chrissie to clean them.

Araminta thought this was a wonderful service and so cheekily put her shoes out too. The next morning, there was a clear message from Chrissie, who had cleaned Richard's and my shoes but left my wife's untouched.

'I don't clean wives' shoes. Serving officers only.'

This was perhaps the first small example for Araminta of what it means to be the spouse of a British Army officer – a role which she was to fulfil splendidly in the coming years. A spouse is absolutely not part of the military machine in any official capacity. Unofficially, however, you are expected to be an accomplished hostess, an expert in military etiquette, a moral compass, a maternal/sisterly shoulder and a social worker.

It is no wonder it took me so long to find the perfect wife.

But I did not keep her all to myself. A few years later, Araminta and I were at a dinner party at which Princess Anne was the guest of honour. The Princess took me to one side during a break in the proceedings.

'Charles – how do you think Araminta would feel about joining my team as a Lady-in-Waiting?'

'I've no idea, Ma'am – but I will ask her.'

'You will do no such thing, Charles. I do my own dirty work!'

She did indeed, and Araminta was delighted to accept.

* * *

Towards the end of my time at Greenwich, I was asked by General Sir David Mostyn to accept the role of Director Military Assistance Overseas (Army), based at the MoD in London, with promotion to the rank of Colonel. He wanted someone gregarious, who was good with people and could turn on the charm, but also be disciplined and diplomatic when necessary. Stop laughing at the back.

We had to leave our accommodation at the College and so we moved in to a flat in London. Araminta was working full-time at Bonhams auction house and, while I was in London, I also worked a Monday-to-Friday week. However, I was overseas for half the time, as I had responsibility for looking after BMATTs (British Military Advisory and Training Teams) stationed around the world, mostly in Africa.

The BMATT in each country consisted of anything from three to twenty officers, and on a visit I would meet with each officer to check how they were getting on. I would also always try to meet with the Ambassador or High Commissioner, the Defence Attaché, and the 'customer', meaning that particular country's senior military commanders, to check they were happy with the training we were providing to their officers.

* * *

One of our largest training deployments was in Nigeria, where we had over twenty officers in total, split into various teams for Armour Training, Artillery Training, Infantry Training and Staff College training. All our people, along with their families, were based in the city of Kaduna.

On one of my visits I was invited to stay with General Paul Omu, whose officers we were training. The General had one of the biggest and most luxurious military houses I had ever seen, complete with permanent staff.

With my usual level of diplomatic tact and subtlety, I gently and sensitively enquired about the domestic fiscal situation.

'Hellfire, General, how can you afford this?'

My host was very candid in his reply.

'Army pay is just my pocket money. I am Garrison Commander – I get 10 per cent of all Garrison contracts, whether it is for food, fuel, maintenance, building works, vehicles, or whatever.'

He saw my eyebrows leap off the top of my head and, with a wide grin, gave me his moral rationalization.

'I am what you British might call the fairy at the top of the Christmas tree. I get all the money and I sprinkle it down. In my tribal area, we have running water, sanitary wells, electricity stations – I pay for it all.'

* * *

On a subsequent visit to Nigeria I had been given orders to try to find out how a number of British-made 'Blowpipe' surface-to-air missile launchers had got into the hands of the Mujahideen in Afghanistan. Several of our training teams in Africa had given instruction on their use, and the Nigerian army had bought quite a few of them. I had an appointment with General Omu at his head office in Lagos to discuss the matter.

His personal secretary met me outside his office and asked me to wait as the General was currently busy. I sat outside, with a cup of tea, while rather strange noises were coming from the General's office. Eventually, things quietened down and a young lady stepped out of the office and walked off, looking rather flushed. The General then appeared with a big grin on his face.

'Colonel Ritchie, sorry to have kept you. I have been doing a little light entertainment, you know.'

I followed the General's example and got straight down to business.

'General Omu, it's about the Blowpipe systems that we supplied to the Nigerian Army. Have you been selling them on?'

The General grinned again.

'Why, Colonel Ritchie, of course I have sold them! Very good weapons, but we don't need them. You will be pleased to know I got a very good price!'

I tried to impress upon the General that the British Army did not look favourably on such activities from nations we tried to give military assistance to. But I knew I was wasting my breath, and there was nothing more I could do about it.

* * *

I was asked to go to the School of Infantry at Warminster to talk to all officers about the British Army's Military Assistance Overseas programme. Leaving London in good time, I was barrelling along the M4 when I came to a grinding halt behind a seemingly endless line of stationary traffic.

I spent the next thirty minutes inching slowly forward before coming to the cause of the delay, which was a minor bump that had closed all but one lane of the motorway, through which the traffic was slowly squeezing.

Once free of the hold-up, but now perilously short of time, I put my foot down and sped along the almost empty carriageway, until the inevitable happened – a flashing blue light appeared in my mirror, and I was pulled over to the side of the road.

The solitary police officer stepped out of his car and approached me, so I wound down my window. As he came up to the car, he actually snapped me a salute.

'Good afternoon, Colonel.'

'Good afternoon, officer. You can tell my rank?'

'Well, Sir, until very recently I was in the Army myself.'

'Really? What regiment?'

'The Green Jackets.'

'Excellent. Who was your commanding officer?'

'Lieutenant Colonel Pringle.'

'Oh, I know him well, he's a good man. How long did you serve?'

I thought if I could keep this up, he might forget why he had stopped me. Fat chance.

'Enough of the chat, Colonel. Why were you speeding?'

I explained the situation, and that due to the delay, I now only had twenty minutes to make my appointment at Warminster, where a large number of officers would be drumming their fingers waiting impatiently for me.

'Right, Sir, I'll take your word for it. So, what I'm going to do is give you an imperial bollocking, and as an ex-Corporal, I'm going to make the most of it. Understood?'

'Yes, officer.'

The young man, chest swollen with pride, then let loose with a tirade of accusations regarding my lack of intelligence, selfishness and dubious parental history, liberally sprinkled with expletives of the most colourful variety.

When he was finished, he gave a huge sigh of satisfaction.

'Thank you, Sir. You cannot imagine how good it feels to give a dressing-down like that to a full Colonel. Now, on your way.'

I made it to Warminster with just seconds to spare. If he had been a Sergeant, I would have been an hour late.

*   *   *

My visits to Zimbabwe were particularly fascinating, as the country was only a few years old in terms of its new constitution and its first President – Robert Mugabe. With hindsight, it is easy to recognize the contributory factors to the issues facing the country today, but even in those early years the danger signs were there.

The leader of our training team in Zimbabwe had been approached by President Mugabe's people with a request that the British Army help the President fulfil one of his major desires, which was to establish the foremost military staff college in Africa as a 'centre of excellence'. Our chap correctly passed the buck to me to deal with.

A meeting with the President was arranged for me, along with Denis Norman, the Minister for Agriculture, who at that time was the only white member of Mugabe's cabinet. The proposed staff college was expected to deal with every aspect of living in Zimbabwe, so that all attendees would have a solid grounding across not just the Army and Air Force but also in things like the police, the prison service, the foreign service – and the country's agriculture.

It soon became obvious why Denis had been invited to the meeting. It was still the early years of Zimbabwean independence and, while quite a number of white farmers had sold up and left the country, the majority of the land was still owned and farmed by white families. The President was very concerned about how the status of land ownership in the newly-independent country would be presented by his 'centre of excellence'.

'Denis – when it comes to discussing agriculture at my college, how are you going to deal with this?'

'Mr President, what will be presented are the facts. We are exporters of food – 36 per cent of our hard currency earnings comes from the sale of agricultural produce to other countries.'

'How will you explain that most of the farmers are of European origin?'

'Mr President, these farmers are just like me – born and bred in Zimbabwe. They are Zimbabweans, the colour of their skin does not affect agriculture.'

I could tell that Denis was dancing a little, but the President pinned him down.

'As part of the college course on agriculture you will ensure that students visit not just a white-owned farm but also a black-owned farm.'

'Of course, Mr President.'

Months later, when the staff college was in operation and training was in full swing, I went out with our training team and Denis Norman himself, to visit a couple of nearby farms.

The first farm we saw was still being run by a 'Zimbo' – i.e. a white Zimbabwean who had embraced the new country's constitution. His farm employed around 150 workers and had an annual turnover equivalent to around US$0.5m. We were given a complete tour of his farm and the workers' accommodation, which included a thriving community centre for his workforce, including a café, a library and even a kindergarten school.

We then went to the farm next door, which prior to independence had been developed and run along identical lines, but had since been sold and was now black-owned. Public spending on education had always been heavily weighted towards the white population, and so very few black people had any skills or training in agriculture. Sadly, but not surprisingly, the farm was in a bad way. Many of the buildings had fallen into disrepair or were completely derelict. Over 80 per cent of the land was not in production. The farming skills required were simply not there.

My relatively limited involvement during the mid-1980s is no qualification to pontificate, but I saw enough glaring evidence that the land reform politics of the time were leading to a huge downward spiral in the country's agricultural economy. This was accelerated when voluntary land sales by white farmers were replaced in the 1990s by compulsory acquisition, then made worse still by the 'fast-track' redistribution policy and related violence.

It seems that only now, following the removal of Robert Mugabe from office in 2017, a more balanced approach is being pursued – over thirty years later, and after so much grief and loss to all involved.

* * *

BMATT Ghana organized a beach barbecue during one of my visits. It was a particularly hot day, and after a few drinks and some food I decided to have a swim to cool off. The sea looked very appealing and remarkably free of other swimmers, sea-snakes or crocodiles pretending to be logs.

Nobody warned me, however, about the rip tides that are very prevalent in the Gulf of Guinea. As I lazily cruised along in the water, I realized that the current had started to take me out to sea. I was initially quite calm – I was a confident swimmer, just a few yards from the beach, so I accepted the challenge that the sea was laying down for me, put my head down and powered manfully against the current.

After about a minute of hard work, I realized I was getting nowhere. In fact, despite my efforts, I was now a few yards further out. I needed to catch my breath, so I flipped on to my back and kicked off with my championship-winning backstroke technique. But I was still drifting away from the beach and I could feel the current getting stronger with every yard I lost.

I turned to the regimental motto of 'Panic with Dignity' and yelled at the top of my lungs, promptly swallowing a hefty dose of seawater. By the time I had spluttered my pipes clear, anyone who had heard my yell had looked around and presumably gone back to their drinks and gossip.

I was now properly scared. I was perhaps only 20 or 25 yards from safety, but the gap was increasing, I was becoming exhausted and I knew I was soon going to be swept beyond the headland and out to sea.

I made one last effort, yelling at the top of my voice and throwing my arms up in the air in the universal sign for 'Damn it, people, I think I'm drowning!' Fortunately, it did the trick. With remarkable speed and ingenuity, given the amount of alcohol that had been consumed already that day, my colleagues, together with various locals, quickly ran to the headland at the end of the beach and formed a human chain into the water by linking arms. The current helped to take the chain out towards me and I was unceremoniously grabbed as I swept past like a waterlogged backpack.

I was returned to dry land and resuscitated with a beer and a burnt sausage, before the inquest began.

'Charles – why on earth were you swimming in one of the most dangerous seas around Africa?'

'I'm sick of flying, so I thought I'd swim back to Lagos. I'd have made it, too, if you buggers hadn't stopped me!'

*　*　*

During my time in DMAO I took a trip to the USA to meet with our US Army colleagues and liaise on various issues relating to our two nations' shared assistance to African countries.

The main event was a meeting in the Pentagon with General Crosbie 'Butch' Saint and a number of his staff. We were discussing the Gambia, and in particular how to help establish a small navy to patrol the coastline. Two patrol boats armed with 0.5-inch machine guns had already been offered by the UK, but there was no naval base from which to operate them.

The General was a good guy. He had done his homework and had an offer to make.

'Colonel Ritchie, we cannot supply personnel, but if you can get permission to deploy a team of British engineers to The Gambia to build the naval base, then the USA will pay the costs to construct and operate it.'

I had been briefed prior to departure by Archie Hamilton, the MoD Minister of State. I had his authority to, in his words 'agree to anything that is sensible'. Getting the funds for a naval base, albeit a very small one, in exchange for the salaries of a team of British Army engineers was definitely sensible.

'Very well, General. As you are willing to pay for the base, I will agree to deploy the engineers to do the work.'

'That's good to hear, Colonel, but please confirm with your line of command before making that commitment.'

'Oh, no need for that, General. I can authorize it.'

There was a brief but uncomfortable silence while the General glowered at me.

'Colonel Ritchie, you need to understand something. This is the United States of America, and the only person authorized to deploy military troops overseas is the President himself!'

'Oh, I see, General. Well, we British leave those sorts of decisions to people like me.'

The poor General went a shade of purple, while his numerous staff suppressed their smirks. But we got the naval base funded by the USA, and the Royal Engineers had a great time living in hotels by the beach, paid for by our American cousins.

*　　*　　*

On one visit to Ghana I accompanied Baroness Lynda Chalker to a reception held at the Presidential Palace by the post-coup President, ex-Flight Lieutenant Jerry Rawlings. I was in full Royal Scots uniform and was approached at one point by a government minister. After a brief exchange of pleasantries, he asked me a loaded question.

'Tell me, Colonel – what do you think of our country?'

I was still new to the job but could vaguely recall something or other that my boss General Mostyn had said about diplomacy. I gave the loaded question my best shot.

'Well, Minister, I think it's quite delightful. I have thoroughly enjoyed myself and have had a most wonderful visit.'

The minister gave a wicked grin.

'Sir, you are a liar!'

'Er … I beg your pardon?'

'You are obviously a liar. You know perfectly well that our country is an absolute tip. Trains don't run, hospitals don't treat, schools don't teach – nothing works.'

'Ah … well …'

'Let me ask you one other question.'

'Yes, Minister?'

'When will you come back to re-colonize us?'

So much for diplomacy.

* * *

I was staying in a hotel in Abidjan on the Ivory Coast. I had a lovely room on the top floor, with a balcony overlooking the beach.

After a very pleasant evening, I went to bed looking forward to a good night's sleep. However, I was rudely woken in the early hours by an almighty bang against the window, so I stumbled over and looked out. Lying on the balcony was the most enormous bat – it must have had a wingspan of almost three feet. In what I suddenly realized was a disgraceful omission on the Army's part, my officer training had not gone into any detail about the taxonomy of bats and, in particular, which ones were of the blood-sucking variety. By the look of this one, it could have downed a few pints and yelled for more.

I rang down to reception to report the airborne assault.

'Yes, Sir, that will be a fruit bat. This often happens, they get tipsy on rotting fruit and lose their way a little.'

'Er … will you remove it?'

'Do not worry, Sir, it will sober up by morning and fly away.'

Relieved that I was not under any immediate vampiric threat, I went back to bed.

In the morning, my uninvited guest was still sleeping off his previous night's antics. I went out on to the balcony and gingerly picked him up, at which point he awoke and started flapping his enormous skinny wings. I let out a less-than-manly shriek and immediately let him fly away, presumably to work on his excuses for the all-nighter before returning to Mrs Fruit Bat.

*   *   *

Lesotho is a tiny country totally surrounded by South Africa. I visited it soon after a military coup. On arrival at the border point between Lesotho and South Africa, near Maseru, we received a welcoming letter from the new military President and had to sign for acceptance of two 9mm automatic pistols loaned to us 'for our safety'.

The Royal Lesotho Defence Force had the youngest recruit I have ever seen. He was around two years of age and had been left at one of the outposts I visited. After he had been born, his mother claimed that one of the soldiers was his father, but she could not remember which one.

In a remarkable show of solidarity and humanity, the soldiers had been looking after the youngster ever since, paying for everything he needed. I managed to organize some clothes and the like for him, via the British High Commission.

*   *   *

While visiting BMATT Swaziland, I was told that the King wanted to see me. I was first met by the British High Commissioner to get briefed. He had no idea why I was being summoned – all he was worried about was the etiquette of meeting the King.

'Now, Colonel, when you enter the room, you must get down and crawl on your hands and knees, to show respect to his Majesty King Mswati.'

'Sorry, but I'm not doing that. I'm wearing the Queen's uniform. I'm not getting down on my knees for anyone.'

That put him in a flap.

'But … what are we going to do? The King has asked to see you, but I can't allow you to disrespect him …'

'Why not arrange for me to be in the room when the King enters, rather than the other way around? I will be sitting low down, below his throne, and will bow as he enters.'

The approach went well, and the King seemed pleased to meet me and expressed satisfaction with the work that our BMATT team was doing with his military personnel. All he wanted to ask was if I could possibly find a retired British officer to be his private secretary, as he wanted someone with training and education.

I promised to do what I could, and within a few weeks we had arranged for a private secretary for the King, through our unofficial internal re-employment system.

* * *

I was on a commercial flight from Mozambique to Mauritius with Max Gandell of the Parachute Regiment. We were approaching our destination when the pilot announced that he was unable to land in Mauritius due to severe crosswinds and so we were diverting to the island of Réunion, about 100 miles south.

We landed and spent a couple of hours at Reunion's little airport, even managing a couple of drinks, before it was announced that the winds had eased a little and so we were going to complete our journey. We took off again, only to discover as we approached Mauritius for the second time, that the winds had actually got stronger.

The pilot then made a more worrying announcement.

'Ladies and gentlemen – it seems our plane was not refuelled in Réunion and so we do not have enough fuel to return there. We are going to have to land on Mauritius one way or another, crosswinds or not.'

The cabin crew did not take the announcement well. One started to cry, panicking the passengers, who were mostly Italian tourists. The co-pilot came to speak to my colleague and me.

'You two don't look like tourists.'

'No – we're British military.'

'RAF?'

'Do we look the types? But he does jump out of planes for a living.'

'OK, can you both come with me.'

The co-pilot led us to the back of the airplane and gave us a quick recap on how to open the rear door and deploy the emergency chute.

'It's going to be a bumpy landing. The plane is very light due to the lack of fuel, and only half the seats are occupied. Take these two empty seats at the back. As soon as you get the chance when we hit the ground, open the door and deploy the chute.'

His last piece of advice was a surprise.

'If anyone tries to leave with their cabin luggage, punch them in the mouth.'

The crosswinds were terrifying, but the pilot did a great job landing the plane, albeit with a mighty thud which broke the undercarriage and ruptured the fuselage. One benefit of almost being out of fuel was that there was much less risk of fire.

There was a modicum of chaos while Max and I got the rear door open and deployed the chute, but once all the other passengers had gone down the chutes, the co-pilot thanked us for our help and allowed us to collect our briefcases and calmly exit via the steps.

I can confirm that no Italian tourists were punched in the process.

*   *   *

Belize was the only country on the other side of the Atlantic with a BMATT, so I did not visit it often. On one occasion, there was nothing particularly out of the ordinary with the training side of things, but I did manage to catch a day's R&R at the end of my trip.

I was out sea-fishing with two colleagues, in a small wooden boat. We hadn't been out long, when the tiny outboard motor spluttered to a halt and refused to re-start. We were only about 100 yards from shore, it was flat calm with no current, and I had my mask and flippers with me, so I decided to tow the boat in to shore, by swimming with its small anchor over my shoulder.

I initially made good progress, encouraged and teased in equal measure by my colleagues, but as we approached the rocky shoreline the waves got a little larger and I was struggling to find a gap in the rocks. After a quick consultation, we decided that if I could get us close enough to the rocks, the little anchor could be used to get us securely moored and we could scramble our way on to the beach from there.

I had just put my head down and started swimming again, with the anchor gripped in one hand ready to throw it into a suitable gap in the rocks, when a reef shark glided in front of me. It must have been around 8ft in length, so not enormous – but easily able to kill a human, especially a slightly smaller-than-average one with tender flanks.

I trod water, watching it through my mask as it circled around the boat and me. My colleagues could see its dorsal fin gliding through the water and so started shouting and splashing to distract it, but it seemed intent on giving me the once-over.

The only thing I could recall regarding shark attacks was the old advice to punch the shark on the nose. I was by no means a boxer – my only attempt at Sandhurst had resulted in getting my own nose broken. Perhaps this was a good omen, if I could do the same to the shark. My left hook couldn't burst the proverbial paper bag, but my right fist was holding the candlestick-sized anchor.

At that moment the reef shark decided to confront me head-on and swam right up to me. It was probably only curious to take a closer look, but I was taking no chances – I whacked it on the snout with the anchor and it shot off like a torpedo.

With adrenalin suddenly pumping, I got rather panicky and, within seconds, had swum up to the rocks, thrown the anchor into a crevice and scrambled out of the water, losing my beloved flippers in the process. I pulled on the anchor rope to bring the boat alongside the rocks, and my colleagues gratefully clambered out, grinning.

'Caught anything today, Charles?'

'Oh, just a tiddler – but he got away.'

Chapter 11

Heavy is the Head that Wears a UN Helmet

My third and final tour of duty in Northern Ireland was as Brigadier in command of The Ulster Defence Regiment (UDR). While this might sound challenging, it was really a desk job, as I had seven battalions each with their own commanding officer, which left me in more of an administrative role.

As a result, I did not gather many entertaining anecdotes from that final tour. Equally, I have no desire to parade any of the more military business end of things in front of you, as this is not that sort of book. Suffice it to say that, sadly, I became only too familiar with attending military funerals.

That said, a return to serve again with the UDR was an honour and a privilege. I did find it strangely amusing that, as their Commander, I automatically became No. 3 on the IRA's death list, after the Secretary for State for Northern Ireland and the Chief Constable of the RUC. Despite this, I had very few close encounters with the IRA. I assume they thought it served them better to leave a bumbling actor in charge of the UDR, rather than try to 'do him in' and risk having a proper hard nut replace him.

* * *

One of the few times I believe I was in genuine danger was while being driven with Angus Ramsay on a tour of the various UDR battalions, during a lengthy handover from me to him at the end of my tour. Approaching a small hump-backed culvert bridge, we could see that a car was coming the other way, so our driver duly slowed down to a crawl, as did the other vehicle. There was just enough room for the cars to pass each other on the bridge, and as we drew alongside we gave a polite wave to the occupants of the other car – who happened to be nuns.

Meeting a car driven by nuns was not a particularly unusual sight on a quiet Irish country road. However, what was more unusual was that, later that day, an IRA bomb was discovered under that very culvert, with a manual detonation device which had obviously not been triggered. We could only assume that whoever had his finger on the trigger had paused, seeing the nuns' car passing us right on the bridge. A minute either way and things could have been very different.

* * *

Once a year, we held an Officers' Study Day in a huge RAF hanger in Ballykelly. I was sitting down to dinner with all 300 officers of the UDR. It had been a busy day, and we were all looking forward to some grub and a few glasses of wine. But before we could start, I looked around to find the chaplain to say grace. But there was no sign of him.

'Where the devil is the chaplain?'

'Ah, sorry, Sir, he could not make it today. But Father O'Reilly is here. He can say grace.'

I took a deep breath and stood up in front of the 90 per cent-plus Protestant crowd.

'Harumph. Er ... Father O'Reilly will now say grace.'

There was a collective intake of breath and an audible furrowing of many Protestant brows. I quickly said my own little prayer that Father O'Reilly would recognize the sensitivity of the situation and not try any sort of recruitment campaign, or worse still call down some punishment from on high for those from the 'other side'.

Father O'Reilly gave me a beaming smile, stood up, steadied himself, and faced the crowd.

'All of you – bow your heads!'

Some of the UDR officers stared back at him, glowering. Father O'Reilly raised his voice and bellowed.

'We are all here in the presence of the Lord. He is not interested in your religious denomination. All of you – BOW YOUR HEADS!'

Everyone grudgingly obeyed. Father O'Reilly then let loose.

'Ohhhhhh Jesus Christ, oh Lord Devine ...

Who turnt the wutter intae wine ...'

He then paused for effect.

'Please forgive us foolish men,
About to turn it back again. Amen.'

The crowd roared with laughter and proceeded to tuck into their dinner, while Father O'Reilly turned to me with a wink. I raised my glass to him, in appreciation of his wisdom and comic timing.

* * *

After my final stint in Northern Ireland, I spent two years in the post of UK National Military Representative (NMR) at Supreme Headquarters Allied Powers Europe (SHAPE), based in Mons in Belgium.

Our accommodation was in a little village called Givry, just outside Mons and very close to the French border. On our first weekend there, Araminta and I were taking a walk around the place to get our bearings. I was also getting used to being able to walk around freely in the open air without a bodyguard constantly at my side, which had been the daily routine in Northern Ireland for the last two years.

I was actually contemplating the fact I had come through my third tour of Northern Ireland unscathed, despite being on the IRA's 'most wanted' list, and was feeling a sense of rather smug satisfaction, when – in one of those bizarre coincidences of life – a motorbike with a Northern Ireland registration plate roared up from behind and screeched to a halt a few yards in front of us.

As the motorcycling killer leapt off his bike and turned to face us, a thought briefly flashed into my mind – how bloody typical of Irish workmen to always show up late! But before I could gather my senses and deal with the imminent threat by panicking or fainting, my attacker spoke up in perfect French.

'*Bonjour monsieur, madame. Où se trouve le garage le plus proche?*'

Flushed with relief, I went to great lengths in my best French to explain that we were new to the area ourselves, we were loving the weather and scenery, the food and the wine, but sadly we had yet to discover where the nearest garage was.

I wanted to enquire about the Northern Irish number plate on his motorcycle, but the young man had clearly more important matters to attend to. He departed in a cloud of dust.

Much to Araminta's annoyance, I spent the rest of the day examining Belgian car registration plates, which all turned out to have exactly the same format (three letters and then three or four digits) as in Northern Ireland.

*   *   *

There was a lot happening in Europe in the summer of 1992. The United Nations were trying to resolve the Croatian War of Independence, Serbia and Montenegro had created the Federal Republic of Yugoslavia, and Bosnia and Herzegovina, Croatia and Slovenia were in the process of joining the UN. If I had been able to look into the future I might have paid more attention to all of this, but I had more pressing matters on my mind – specifically, getting the booze for the SHAPE party which we Brits were going to give for the Queen's Birthday.

The Belgians, in their wisdom, levied a very high tax on alcohol, and Belgian customs officers were kept very busy on the border with neighbouring France, where drink was even cheaper than we could buy it in the NAAFI. This had suddenly become a serious issue, as the cost of the champagne was likely to blow the whole party budget, which was funded by contributions from all the British military officers at SHAPE.

However, my little village of Givry was only a mile or two from the French border. A quiet little country road led from France to Givry, with no border check. You were met with a simple 'Welcome to Belgium' sign, along with a warning that the road should not be used to transport any duty-payable goods and that the Belgian customs authorities performed regular checks on road-users.

A colleague and I decided we needed to mount an upscale operation in order to procure fifteen cases of French champagne that clearly would not pass as 'for personal use'. We hired a van, drove it over the border, bought our champagne and then deployed the approach I learnt from the IRA's method of smuggling arms across the Irish border. I headed off down the little country road back to Givry in my own car, followed at a distance by my colleague in the van, with the agreement that if I spotted a customs check I would simply stop the car and put my hazard lights on, to warn my colleague to turn back.

Fortunately, we had a clear road for our short trip and soon got back to my house, where we stored the drink in my garage until the night of the party – which went very well indeed, thanks in some part to copious helpings of French champagne.

*   *   *

My opposite number in the US Army had the common habit of greeting you every day and asking how you were, but then walking on without waiting for an answer. We therefore fell into a terrible charade: he would ask how I was and I would simply say, 'Fine, thanks, how are you?', but would get no answer as he had already moved on.

This became quite exasperating. Many years as a British Army officer had given me a very strong desire to chatter about inane nonsense with anyone and everyone I met, in order to sound intelligent and pass the time of day, while avoiding real work.

One morning as I saw him approaching, I decided I needed to 'lance the boil', so to speak.

'Hi Charles, how are you today?'

As he continued to stride past me, I caught him by the arm, causing him to spin around with a shocked look on his face. I finally had his attention.

'Listen here, my dear fellow. You are polite enough to ask me every day how I am. Not once have I ever had the courtesy to reply, properly and accurately.'

'Er ...'

'I must make amends for my rudeness and so would like you to know that I have the following wrong with me: my back is sore from all the heavy desk work; I have tennis elbow and housemaid's knee although I've not played with a racquet or a housemaid for years; my trigger finger is itchy and my nylon socks have given me trench foot; and I have a constant pain in my neck from a boil that badly needs lanced.'

Bless him, he clearly thought I was at death's door or, at the very least, highly contagious, for he mumbled some apology and sped off. From that day on, he only said 'Hello' and never again asked me how I was.

*   *   *

I reached my fiftieth birthday while in Belgium. Shocked and surprised at having successfully stayed alive for so long, I decided to throw a big party to celebrate this milestone, on the assumption I might not reach sixty. I invited a lot of friends to come over to Belgium, and it was wonderful that many of them made the trip.

It proved to be a great success. Well, I enjoyed it immensely, anyway. I was surprised and delighted that the Princess Royal came, despite her always-packed diary. She brought her daughter Zara, who was nine or ten years old at the time and who charmed everyone by greeting them at the door as they arrived.

It was a very informal party, which I think the Princess appreciated. We had a great laugh at the expense of one of my colleagues, Peter Williams (now Major General retired, so he'll probably get me shot for telling this story). Peter had arrived a little late and seemed a bit distracted as he said hello. The Princess happened to be standing with me at the time, so I introduced Peter, who shook her hand absent-mindedly and then immediately asked where the bar was. As he strode off in the direction I pointed, we could hear the loudly-whispered conversation between Peter and his wife Anne.

'Peter! Don't you know who that is …?'

'No, dammit – who?'

'That's Princess Anne!'

'Oh my God, really? Oh no … Oh damn … Oh hell …'

The Princess and I had a good giggle. I briefly considered giving her a tray of canapés to offer to arriving guests, but then thought better of it.

* * *

I hoped that my final gig before retirement was to be as Military Attaché to the British Embassy in Paris. However, I received a rather disturbing phone call one evening from the Deputy Military Secretary to the MoD, Major General Johnny Hall.

'Charles Ritchie – I assume you have a drink in your hand. Put it down, I have something to tell you.'

'Yes, Sir?'

'You have been selected by the Chief of Defence Staff to go on tour as Chief of Staff to the United Nations Protection Force in Yugoslavia.'

'But what about my posting to Paris as Military Attaché?'

'That'll have to wait for six months.'

This was a blow. An unaccompanied six-month tour, at my time of life, to a stressful UN posting, was honestly not terribly appealing. I started wriggling.

'Sir, if I may ask – why me?'

'The UNPROFOR Commander doesn't speak English. You're the only bugger we can find that speaks his lingo.'

Then a possible escape route appeared.

'Now, Charles – you'll have to have an interview with this French General, so make a good impression, won't you. There's no one else left in the damn barrel, we don't want to have to offer the post to the bloody Americans.'

British Army man-management at its very best.

* * *

My interview with the wonderful General Jean Cot, Commander of UNPROFOR in Zagreb, did not go as planned. I had come armed with my most potent, fully recoiling Franglais, which I was going to fire from the hip at every opportunity. But the General sat down opposite me, opened up his diary and asked me just one question. When could I start?

I wracked my brains trying to come up with a genuine but ridiculous excuse that might put the kibosh on this posting. I suddenly had an inspirational flash which made me quite giddy – The Royal Scots were due to provide the Queen's Royal Guard at Balmoral that year.

With a deep breath, I explained to the General in my best French that, as Honorary Colonel of the Regiment, I couldn't possibly start until after the annual Balmoral Guard Cocktail Party.

The General didn't blink. He calmly wrote the date in his diary, welcomed me to his team and congratulated me on being the only officer he had ever met who planned his army career around cocktail parties.

* * *

One part of my job was to visit all the contributing nations' military deployments, to discuss and try to resolve issues, as well as (occasionally) handing out a rollocking if they weren't behaving themselves or doing what they were told.

Most of these visits were pretty routine, but the Russian officers all seemed to know that I had worked previously in BRIXMIS – and what that had involved. They automatically assumed that I spoke Russian and so, whenever I met up with any of them, they would start babbling away in their own language and I would have to ask them to please speak English as I didn't speak Russian. This would invariably be met with the same smile and knowing wink I used to get in East Germany. Bless them, they thought I was still maintaining some sort of cover.

However, over time I did eventually get them to realize that, indeed, I really could not speak Russian. This was not a problem for the job, as most of them had excellent English. One officer in particular had a cut-glass accent that suggested he had been schooled at Eton.

I found having Russian troops to deploy was particularly helpful for UNPROFOR. On one occasion, we sent the Russians to Sarajevo to stop the Serbs from shelling the area. The Serbs typically would not pay any attention to UN requests, but we found they would at least listen to the Russians in UN uniform.

* * *

The most difficult problem that General Cot faced during his command of UNPROFOR was getting access to sufficient military resources to do the protection job properly. This was exacerbated by the UN pen-pushers in New York repeatedly declaring 'UN Safe Areas' without first consulting the forces on the ground and, in particular, providing the means of securing such areas. Srebrenica was the first – and worst – example.

Srebrenica was declared a UN Safe Area in April 1993, five months before I took up the post of Chief of Staff. We eventually got a small Dutch battalion (known as 'DUTCHBAT') in place in Srebrenica early in 1994 to replace an even smaller Canadian force. However, it was clear to us that the lightly equipped and inexperienced Dutch troops would be ineffective if faced with a serious assault on the area by Serbian forces. Yet repeated requests for more military resources were falling on deaf ears.

General Cot was about to come to the end of his time as UNPROFOR commander. On 4 March 1994, he called me into his office and ordered me to send a signal direct to Kofi Annan at UN HQ in New York. While confirming the successful handover of the Srebrenica Safe Area from the Canadians to the Dutch, I ensured that the signal pulled no punches in stating what a risk the UN was taking in not providing a more substantial force. The key elements read as follows.

> I cannot emphasise too strongly that it is the considered opinion of this headquarters that declaring Srebrenica to be a 'United Nations Safe Area' is extremely unwise without giving us the military resources to guarantee this.
>
> With the greatest respect to DUTCHBAT, they are lightly equipped without any heavy weapons and early reports indicate they are not sufficiently trained and would be incapable of defending the Safe Area against a determined, well equipped Serbian Force supported by armour and artillery.
>
> **At the risk of repeating myself I must emphasise that to guarantee Srebrenica as a Safe Area an armoured brigade with 2 Battalions of armoured infantry, a tank regiment and an artillery regiment equipped with self-propelled artillery is required.**
>
> Signed – CDM Ritchie, Brigadier, Chief of Staff, UNPROFOR

There followed various claims and promises, but this very clear request was never met. Following General Cot's departure, I left my post in Zagreb a few weeks later. The Dutch force was left under-resourced and unsupported for a further year, until finally the Bosnian Serbs, commanded by General Mladic, intimidated and overran the Dutch unit and went on to perpetrate the Srebrenica genocide of over 8,000 Bosniak men and boys.

I do not wish to dwell on this appalling tragedy. It has been much written about and debated since, including a lengthy investigation by the Dutch which resulted in the resignation of their entire cabinet. I will simply state that, in my opinion, the Dutch were put in an impossible position by the inability of the UN to provide adequate resources, despite the very clear and direct warnings repeatedly given by UNPROFOR for over a year prior. If the proper measures had been taken by the UN in New York, I am convinced that the Srebrenica genocide would never have happened.

*   *   *

Before my final visit to the Russian battalion, their commanding officer invited me to address his men, so I decided to play a game with them.

By this stage, the Russians had accepted the fact that I couldn't speak their language, so I asked my Eton-educated Russian friend to assist me in translating my short address speech into Russian and writing it out phonetically for me. I had an obtained a decent ear for the accent from my time in Potsdam, so I dusted off my acting skills and learnt my lines by heart.

On the day, I addressed the whole Russian battalion in half-decent Russian. Several officers let their jaws drop, and I could practically hear their thoughts – 'That little Scottish madman was double-bluffing us all the time!'

After the speeches, I was shown around their base and invited to drive one of their massive 8-wheel APCs, which was great fun. As I climbed down after my drive, I expressed my thanks, stating that I'd photographed several of these in my time but had never been invited to drive one, which got howls of knowing laughter. There was then a terrific party in the evening and we all got suitably, outrageously drunk.

Chapter 12

Out, Out Brief Candle

The final posting of my Army career, to the frazzled relief of my superiors, was as Military Attaché in Paris. What nonsense could Ritchie possibly get up to in such a gentle environment? Two different men held the role of Her Majesty's Ambassador to France during my time there. Sir Christopher Mallaby, a fine diplomat, suffered my arrival towards the end of his tenure, although I refute all suggestions that my behaviour drove him out. His successor, Sir Michael Jay, arrived with a reputation for not suffering fools. I can hear his exasperated sighs even now.

* * *

Formal dinners usually have a detailed seating plan, but on one particularly grand occasion, each guest was allocated to a table but not an individual seat. As a result, there were no place-cards on the table for me to squint at. Worse, Araminta was seated on another table so couldn't helpfully whisper to me the names of any unrecognized guests.

As I approached my table, I saw that everyone else was already seated, so I sat down in the one spare seat. In my best French, I turned and introduced myself to the lady sat immediately to my right, whom I did not recognize.

'Good evening, Madame, I am Brigadier Charles Ritchie, Military Attaché at the British Embassy.'

'Good evening … I am the Comtesse de Paris.'

I had not previously met Her Royal Highness Princess Isabelle, the Comtesse de Paris, and so I expressed my delight at making her acquaintance. We then exchanged pleasantries before I turned to the lady sitting on my left, to repeat the process.

'Good evening, Madame, I am Brigadier Charles Ritchie, Military Attaché at the British Embassy.'

'Good evening.'

Hmm. Bit of a cold fish, I thought. But I was not going to be put off.

'Madame, may I have the honour of knowing whom I am sitting next to?'

'Please don't worry who I am.'

This rather terse rebuff brought the table to an immediate hush. Eight pairs of eyes were staring at me in stunned silence.

Confused but undeterred, I turned back to the shy lady on my left.

'Madame, my sincere apologies, but I would really like to know ...'

She gave a gentle sigh.

'Well, if you must ... I am Madame Chirac, wife of the President of France.'

I froze in horror. Thankfully, Madam Chirac then had the good grace to smile at my reaction, and there were giggles from around the table at the blundering Brit who hadn't recognized the most famous woman in France.

* * *

National Service in the UK ended in 1962, soon after I was commissioned. No need to thank me.

However, in France it was still in place as late as 1996. At the time, young men aged eighteen still had to give ten months of service, but the French had decided to review this matter again, as their military had struggled to deploy sufficient trained units during the First Gulf War.

As part of their review process, the French Senate were debating the issue, and the British Embassy was asked for a representative from the UK to appear before them and share our experiences and views. The Ambassador was not a military man himself but he had an irritating new Military Attaché to keep occupied. I was therefore chosen to attend, especially as I was old enough to have personally served during the last days of British National Service.

Dressed in my full military regalia, I appeared before the French Senate in the Luxembourg Palace. I was told this was the first time that a serving British officer had ever done so. I duly delivered the official written statement supplied to me by the MoD, which of course was a very balanced and even-handed one, and so terribly boring.

I was therefore delighted when I was asked by one of the Senators for my personal view, given my own experiences.

'Well, gentlemen … I believe national servicemen are valuable when your professional army is in action overseas, as they can offer some protection to your homeland. But my view is that, while National Service is a great cultural bonding exercise, it is in military terms nothing more than a uniformed youth club.'

That actually got a chuckle and a small round of applause from my audience, and only a few frowns.

France suspended military conscription a few months later, before going on to end it formally by law. Sadly, the volume of thank-you letters I have since received from the young men of France has been distinctly underwhelming. I should have left a forwarding address.

*   *   *

I was attending a formal dinner in the Embassy. At the Ambassador's request, each of the senior members of the Embassy was usually asked to host a different table of guests. On this occasion, I was told rather pointedly that I had to be on my best behaviour and, in particular, I was told, 'No jokes about the French language'.

The reason for my card being so explicitly marked was that one of the guests at my table was the Secretary of the Académie Française, the council responsible for maintaining the standard and integrity of the French language. The Académie has existed for centuries, having been set up by Cardinal Richelieu on behalf of Louis XIII, and is a very grand and – dare I say – rather pretentious body. For example, its forty life members are known as *Les Immortels*. In recent times it has been accused of becoming ever more conservative and reactionary in the face of perceived dilution of the French language by anglicization.

During dinner, I played the polite host for as long as I could. But the third glass of wine stirred my patriotism, and I felt my country was depending on me. The opportunity came when my distinguished guest made an appreciative comment about this rather large prawn (*'cette crevette'*) that he was tucking in to. I grabbed the prawn by the horn.

'Monsieur Secretary, my French is far from perfect, but don't you mean *'ce crevette'*?

He paused with his fork in mid-air and stared at me.

'I'm sorry?'

'Well, Monsieur Secretary, it is obviously a male prawn. I can clearly see its sports equipment …'

The other guests giggled at the cheek of this Brit teasing the chief *Immortel*, but the old fellow did not realize I had my tongue firmly in my cheek. He helped himself to a little umbrage along with his *beurre blanc* sauce.

'You British and Americans, you are always ready to ridicule the beautiful French language. But you are responsible for its pollution!'

'I do apologize, Monsieur Secretary. What sort of pollution do you mean?'

'*Jogging … week-end … marketing …* and that horrible Americanism – *okay*. Urgh!'

'But, Monsieur Secretary, with great respect, 'okay' is of French origin!'

He choked on his Sauvignon.

'What? Of course not! It is American, and it is terrible!'

I then presented the Secretary with the benefit of my dubious wisdom.

'Monsieur Secretary – I believe 'okay' originates from the time when New Orleans was part of the French colony of Louisiana. When bales of freshly picked cotton were gathered, the landowners checked them for quality, as only the best were sent to the coast for export to France. They would walk along the row of cotton bales, calling out their instructions – either '*Au quai!*' ('To the harbour!') if the bale was good enough for export to the motherland, or simply '*Non!*' if it was for local sale. Hence '*au quai*' became a common term in the Americas for anything good or agreeable.'

To give him credit, Monsieur Secretary received this cotton-picking bombshell with good humour.

'Well, well, I did not know that. It is always the case at these sorts of occasions, that you can learn something new.'

We then spent a very jolly evening in each other's company, although I never did learn why *le weekend* is male but *une interview* is female.

* * *

Despite teasing Monsieur Secretary of the Académie Française about his native tongue, I have to say how much I love the French language, despite not being fluent myself – although I have once been accused of being effluent.

Being able to communicate in French has helped me many times throughout my career, and spending three years in Paris honed my skill and confidence considerably. It has also proved very valuable since my retirement from the Army. As Secretary of The New Club in Edinburgh I was very fortunate, along with several others, to have lunch at the Club with Sean Connery and his wonderful wife Micheline. It was the day that he received his knighthood from Her Majesty The Queen at Holyrood Palace in July 2000 and so was a special day for him. To share in just a small part of it was a great thrill for me.

I could tell, however, that Micheline was struggling a little with all the strange Scottish accents around the lunch table – no other Scot sounds quite like her husband, no matter what the world might think! I therefore struck up a conversation with her in her native French, which she greatly appreciated, as did the great man himself.

Inevitably, I also regaled the table with a couple of stories from my past, including my trips across the 'Bridge of Spies'. I was charmed and delighted when Sir Sean turned to me at the end of the meal.

'You know, Charles, thanks to the Bond films, people sometimes confuse me with him, even though I am just an actor playing a part. It is wonderful for me to meet someone who truly was a spy for real!'

With that, he shook me warmly by the hand. What a charming man.

*   *   *

France's national Gendarmerie is one of two police forces but, unlike the national Police Force, the Gendarmerie is a branch of the Armed Forces. I was therefore the official British liaison officer to the Gendarmerie and would occasionally be invited to functions and meetings with them.

I was attending a day-long conference at the Gendarmerie HQ, attended by over 200 gendarmes of various ranks. One of the responsibilities of the Gendarmerie is crowd management at public gatherings and demonstrations, particularly if it turns into riot control. I therefore found myself chatting to a few officers over coffee about my experiences in Northern Ireland. They all expressed great interest in the British use of plastic bullets for riot control – something which they did not have access to, having to rely on tear gas or live ammunition.

The topic of equipment was on the conference agenda for discussion, including the possible introduction of the use of plastic bullets to the Gendarmerie. The most senior officers expressed reluctance, but I was invited to share my view based on my experiences, which in summary was that they are as effective but obviously much less extreme than live rounds, but also much more effective than tear gas.

After a brief Q&A, there was a call for a simple show of hands among the conference attendees on the idea of obtaining British plastic bullets and guns for riot control. Well over 80 per cent of the attendees raised their hands in favour.

This led to a number of formal meetings in the following weeks at which I liaised between the senior officers of the Gendarmerie and our Defence Procurement chaps, helping to explain how we used the bullets, the special guns needed to fire them, what training was required, the costs, etc. After a lot of initial scepticism, the Gendarmerie finally bit the rubber bullet and placed an initial order for over £3m of equipment.

My commission for brokering the deal was a simple pat on the back, but I genuinely felt satisfaction that I had a very direct influence on the introduction of less lethal weapons to the streets of France.

*   *   *

I met His Majesty King Olav V of Norway when he paid a visit to France in his role as Colonel-in-Chief of the Green Howards. The King's father had held the same ceremonial position since the Green Howards had fought alongside the Norwegian Army during the Nazi invasion of Norway in 1940.

The King's trip included the unveiling of a memorial in Crepon on the Normandy Coast to the 6th and 7th Battalions and specifically to Company Sergeant Major Stanley Hollis, who won the only Victoria Cross to be awarded on D-Day.

I found the King to be a charming gentleman and very chatty. During a lull in the proceedings, he asked me if I had any connections to Norway.

'As a matter of fact, your Majesty, yes I do.'

'Oh, really?'

'Yes. My Aunt Dawn married a Norwegian Army officer whom she met when he was stationed near our home in Scotland during the war.'

'Wonderful! What is his name?'

'His name was Colonel Eric Prydz.'

The King laughed loudly.

'Amazing! Your uncle was my first Commanding Officer. He taught me how to ride!'

'Well I never!'

'Are your aunt and uncle still alive?'

'The Colonel sadly died a few years ago, but my aunt still lives in Norway, although she is due to return to Scotland soon due to ill-health.'

It was a lovely surprise for the whole family when we heard a few weeks later that the King had arranged a farewell reception at the Royal Palace in Oslo for Aunt Dawn, which she absolutely loved.

*   *   *

The Ambassador received an invitation to a St Andrew's Day party at the French Officers' Club. He was unable to go, so I was delighted to attend in his place – in my Royal Scots mess kit, but in the role of representing the Ambassador, rather than as a Scottish military officer.

There were about eighty attendees, mostly French but some Scots and a few English, and it was a terrific evening at which the single malt flowed liberally. When it came to the toasts, I duly proposed a toast to Her Majesty the Queen, which was well received by all. Flushed with success and the water of life, I thought it would then be an excellent idea, given the circumstances, to propose a very particular toast.

'Gentlemen, as this is an important night for Scotland, and we are being entertained here in the capital of France … please be upstanding and raise your glasses to the oldest military alliance in the world, between France and Scotland, against our traditional and mutual enemy, the English. *La Vieille Alliance!*'

To much laughter and cheering, we toasted the Auld Alliance.

I spent the next day in the recovery position but on Monday morning was summoned to see the Ambassador. Apparently, one of Saturday night's guests had been upset by my toast and had handed in a letter of complaint. The Ambassador was not amused and tore me off a strip, reminding me that I had been representing him as the *British* Ambassador to France and had no right to be toasting Scottish wars against the English. He was, of course, correct, and I apologized.

But I would still like to meet the humourless sod who wrote that letter.

*   *   *

I was attending *La Fête Nationale,* known outside of France as 'Bastille Day', during which a huge military parade takes place on the Champs-Élysées. I had somehow finagled myself into a line-up of very distinguished guests who were being introduced to President Chirac. As I warmly shook the President's hand, an elegant voice called out in perfect English from the President's left.

'Ah, Brigadier Ritchie – perhaps you can remember who I am?'

It was, of course, Madam Chirac, who gave me a warm forgiving smile as she took my hand. Classy lady.

*   *   *

Saturday, 30 August 1997. I was one week away from retiring from the British Army.

It was my last weekend stint on call as duty officer for the British Embassy. After a quiet day, I went out for dinner with my son Paul, along with my nephew and a friend of his who had come to visit for a few days. After dinner we were walking home when we saw a crowd of paparazzi gathered outside the front of the Ritz Hotel.

'Wow, Dad, look – what's going on?'

'Oh, it's probably Elton John or somebody like that, staying at the hotel.'

We were heading off to a little Irish pub I knew, so Araminta came to meet us to take Paul home. She broke the news about who was at the Ritz.

'Guess what, dear – Princess Diana and Dodi Al-Fayed are in Paris!'

'Oh shit!'

I was immediately concerned. Neither I nor anyone else at the British Embassy had been told. If we had known in advance, as is usual for VIP visits, we would have arranged overt and/or covert personal security, transport cars and chase cars, known drivers, etc.

However, as we passed the front of the hotel, I noticed two Range Rovers parked immediately outside – one British-registered, the other French, each with a driver and a PPO (Personal Protection Officer) inside. Relieved that something had been organized already, albeit without my knowing, there was nothing more I could do that evening, so Araminta and Paul went back to our apartment, and the rest of us went on to the pub.

Little did I realize at the time that, during the Stevens Inquiry several years later, I would be interviewed quite aggressively by the British police.

'Brigadier Ritchie – you were the duty officer at the British Embassy on 30 August?'

'Yes.'

'You discovered that evening that Princess Diana was staying at the Ritz Hotel?'

'Yes.'

'Yet you did nothing about it?'

'No – at the time, there was nothing I could do.'

'Brigadier Ritchie, we have been to your apartment. From the balcony that overlooks the Rue Cambon, could you see the back door of the Ritz Hotel?'

'Yes.'

'Could you have seen Princess Diana leave the Ritz by that back door?'

'If I was there. But I was not at home that evening.'

Then it got a touch more difficult.

'Brigadier Ritchie – you have worked with MI6 in the past, is that correct?'

'Yes.'

'We also believe you are a member of the Royal Household, yes?'

'Yes.'

'We also understand that in August 1980, you knowingly and deliberately caused the death of two men in a traffic accident in East Germany.'

'Well, no, it was not like that at all …'

'Brigadier Ritchie, you were outside the front of the Ritz hotel in the hour before Princess Diana's death. Your apartment overlooks the rear of the hotel, so you had the means to know exactly when she left …'

I could see where this was going. In their minds, I had 'previous'. They were implying that I was the one tasked with arranging Princess Diana's death via a road traffic accident, at the request of the Royal Household via MI6.

Thankfully, I had witnesses to confirm my whereabouts at the time of the accident, including the landlord of the pub who knew I worked at the Embassy and remembered me that particular evening, because I had arrived with two very good-looking young men!

It was, of course, simply a terrible accident – but one that could have been avoided. Much has been written about Henri Paul, the driver who worked for the Ritz Hotel and was at the wheel of the Mercedes when it crashed. He was already off-duty on that fateful night and had indeed been drinking at the hotel bar, as was widely reported.

It was Dodi Al-Fayed's father who decided that the couple should not leave in the two arranged Range Rovers in front of the assembled paparazzi but should instead be driven away from the back door of the hotel by Henri Paul. If only they had left by the front of the hotel, pausing to give a few pictures to the assembled cameramen, and been driven away by the waiting Range Rovers – as recommended by their security staff.

*   *   *

The first I knew about that terrible accident was at 5.00am the following morning, when the Canadian Defence Attaché rang me. I immediately went into the Embassy, where all the staff were gathering. I spent most of the next 48 hours on the phone making all manner of arrangements, from books of condolence to organizing the bearer-party that would take the Princess's body back to the UK.

We set up a guard of honour in the room where the open coffin had been laid. She looked simply beautiful. It is a terribly well-worn cliché, but I have no words other than to say that it was as if she was simply lying asleep.

Sir Michael Jay arrived with Prince Charles, along with the Princess's brother and sisters. After their visit, the RAF bearer-party sergeant came to me.

'Sir – I need your help to tie the straps down in the coffin.'

He and I duly applied the straps, which were necessary for the journey, and the coffin lid was then sealed. The sergeant then asked me a difficult question.

'Sir – what flag is to be draped over the coffin – the Union Flag?'

Of course, he was right that the formally correct answer was the Union Flag, as the Princess was no longer an active serving member of the Royal Family. But that simply did not seem right to me. I had seen the unfair criticism that the press had been laying at the door of the Royal Family in the immediate aftermath of the accident. Using the Union Flag would have given the press more ammunition. I let my heart rule my head.

'She is the mother of the future King. Put on the Royal Standard.'

'Are you sure, Sir?'

'Yes. I'll take full responsibility. I retire from the Army next week anyway – what's the worst they can do to me?'

The next day, I was given a right royal rollocking by a Palace jobsworth. I have had many tellings-off during my career, but this was the one that really upset me. It had all been a terrible, appalling tragedy, and everyone's emotions, mine included, had been shredded. I hated the idea that I might have made it ever so slightly worse for the Royal Family by my snap decision.

But the following Wednesday, a courier arrived at the Embassy with a letter addressed to the Ambassador. He came to find me straight away and kindly showed the letter to me. It was from the Palace and, without wishing to divulge any details, it asked him to thank me for my 'unconventional decision' regarding the Royal Standard.

My selfish upset was an irrelevance in the circumstances of the whole tragic event. Nevertheless, the thought that such a considerate communication was sent during a time of such sadness has always meant a great deal to me.

I had given Sir Michael a few causes for consternation and heartburn during my time in Paris but, gentleman that he is, he let me gather myself for a moment. He then spoke with a smile and a twinkle in his eye.

'Charles, you really are the most unconventional soldier.'

'Yes, Sir. Thank you.'

Acknowledgements

With thanks to all the incredible people that Charles met during his military career. It was his love and respect for you all that gave his adventures such wonderful humanity and soul.

Enormous thanks go to Graeme MacArthur, great friend and neighbour, without whom this book would not have been written, and to all at Pen & Sword Books for their sterling work and kind support.

Also thanks to Ash Lyons, who digitized Charles' old albums for the book's photographs: www.ashlyonsphoto.com

Charles loved life and people and with his book now published he will live on in his stories for ever and bring huge enjoyment to all those who read it.

Araminta Ritchie